The HUMONGOUS BOOK of PRESCHOOL IDEAS

Group

Loveland, Colorado

www.group.com

Group resources really work!

This Group resource incorporates our R.E.A.L. approach to ministry. It reinforces a growing friendship with Jesus, encourages long-term learning, and results in life transformation, because it's

Relational
Learner-to-learner interaction enhances learning and builds Christian friendships.

Experiential
What learners experience through discussion and action sticks with them up to 9 times longer than what they simply hear or read.

Applicable
The aim of Christian education is to equip learners to be both hearers and doers of God's Word.

Learner-based
Learners understand and retain more when the learning process takes into consideration how they learn best.

THe HumoNGoUS BooK of PReSCHooL IDeas

Visit our website: **group.com**

Credits
Chief Creative Officer: Joani Schultz
Children's Senior Developer: Patty Anderson
Children's Ministry Champion: Christine Yount Jones
Copy Editor: Dena Twinem
Project Managers: Jan Kershner and Scott M. Kinner
Art Director: Andrea Filer
Print Production Artist: Greg Longbons
Cover Designer/Illustrator: Illustrated Alaskan Moose
Interior Illustrator: Andrea Filer
Production Manager: DeAnne Lear

Unless otherwise indicated, all Scripture quotations are taken from the *Holy Bible*, New Living Translation, copyright © 1996, 2004. Used by permission of Tyndale House Publishers, Inc., Carol Stream, Illinois 60188. All rights reserved.

Library of Congress Cataloging-in-Publication Data
The humongous book of preschool ideas. -- 1st American pbk. ed.
    p. cm.
 ISBN 978-0-7644-3601-7 (pbk. : alk. paper) 1. Church work with children. 2. Bible stories, English. 3. Preschool children--Religious life. I. Group Publishing.
 BV639.C4H84 2008
 268'.432--dc22
                    2007038351

ISBN 978-0-7644-3601-7

10 9 8   17 16 15 14
Printed in the United States of America.

Contents

Introduction...5

Old Testament

1. GOD MADE THE WORLD (Genesis 1:1-31)...................................7

2. GOD MADE PEOPLE (Genesis 1:26-31; 2:4-25)..........................16

3. NOAH AND THE ARK (Genesis 6:5–8:13).................................24

4. JOSEPH TELLS HIS DREAMS (Genesis 37:1-11)..........................33

5. JOSEPH IS SOLD INTO SLAVERY (Genesis 37:12-36)...................39

6. JOSEPH FORGIVES HIS BROTHERS (Genesis 42:1–45:28)............44

7. MOSES MEETS GOD AT THE BURNING BUSH (Exodus 2:11–3:20)......50

8. MOSES PLEADS WITH PHARAOH (Exodus 7:14–12:31).................56

9. MOSES CROSSES THE RED SEA (Exodus 13:17–14:31).................63

10. JERICHO'S WALLS COME DOWN (Joshua 6:1-27)......................69

11. RUTH TRUSTS GOD (Ruth 1–4)..75

12. SAMUEL LISTENS TO GOD (1 Samuel 3:1-21)...........................80

13. DAVID BECOMES KING (1 Samuel 16:1-13)..............................84

14. DAVID DEFEATS GOLIATH (1 Samuel 17:1-50)..........................88

15. DAVID AND JONATHAN ARE FRIENDS (1 Samuel 18:1-4; 19:1-7; 20:1-42)...............92

16. ELIJAH CHALLENGES THE PROPHETS OF BAAL (1 Kings 18:16-39)......97

17. ELISHA HELPS A WIDOW AND HER SONS (2 Kings 4:1-7)............103

18. JOSIAH DISCOVERS GOD'S WORD (2 Chronicles 34:1-33).........109

19. NEHEMIAH REBUILDS THE WALL (Nehemiah 2:11–6:19)...........117

20. DANIEL IS SAFE IN THE LIONS' DEN (Daniel 6:1-23)................123

New Testament

21. GOD TELLS PEOPLE TO GET READY (Isaiah 9:6; Jeremiah 33:14-16; Luke 3:7-18) 131

22. JESUS IS BORN (Luke 1:26-45; 2:1-20) 140

23. JESUS GROWS UP (Luke 2:39-52) 148

24. JESUS CALLS THE DISCIPLES (Mark 1:16-20) 154

25. JESUS TURNS WATER INTO WINE (John 2:1-11) 161

26. JESUS CLEARS THE TEMPLE TO WORSHIP GOD (John 2:13-22) 167

27. JESUS EXPLAINS ETERNAL LIFE TO NICODEMUS (John 3:1-21) 173

28. JESUS TALKS WITH A SAMARITAN WOMAN (John 4:4-26) 181

29. JESUS BLESSES THE CHILDREN (Mark 10:13-16) 184

30. JESUS TELLS ABOUT A GOOD SAMARITAN (Luke 10:25-37) 189

31. JESUS HEALS A BLIND MAN (Mark 10:46-52) 194

32. JESUS NOTICES A WIDOW'S GIVING (Mark 12:41-44) 200

33. JESUS ENTERS JERUSALEM (Matthew 21:1-11) 205

34. JESUS WASHES THE DISCIPLES' FEET (John 13:1-17) 210

35. JESUS CAME TO DIE FOR US (Luke 19:28-40; 23:1-49) 212

36. THE ANGEL FREES PETER FROM JAIL (Acts 12:1-18) 216

37. LYDIA IS CONVERTED (Acts 16:9-16) 220

Introduction

Welcome to the humongous resource with humongous ideas to make a humongous impact in kids' lives!

Preschool children learn in many different ways. Some understand through visual crafts they create. Others learn through movement during games. And another group learns best through music and motions.

This book gives you all kinds of humongous ideas for all these learners.

No matter the Bible story and life lesson, little children need different ways to actively explore God's Word and learn life-transforming truth. And you need easy ways to quickly find those age-appropriate, sensory-filled learning experiences.

That's why you've picked up the right resource!

Humongous *ideas.* This book is full of humongous-impact Bible stories, from the Old Testament to the New. Each Bible story uses active-learning where preschoolers actually become part of the story as they sing, dance, make sound effects, or cheer to bring the Bible story to life. After the story, you'll find a variety of humongous ideas that will help children remember the story and apply it to their lives.

Humongous *learning.* Every activity uses an active learning approach, helping kids learn in their unique ways. Whether it's a surprise in a Bible experience, the excitement of a game, or the creativity of a craft, little children will dig deeper into the story and the corresponding truth with the opportunity for humongous learning!

Humongous *life change.* Children will remember the Bible stories and life applications because you've chosen the humongous ideas that work for your children, for your setting, and for the message you want to share. As a result, children will grow in their relationships with Jesus.

Easy to do! Each story is followed by humongous activity ideas, divided into easy-to-find categories. After each story, you'll find most or all of these categories: Bible Experiences, Crafts, Games, Prayers, Snacks, and Songs. Use the story as your foundation, then grow your preschool learning experience from there!

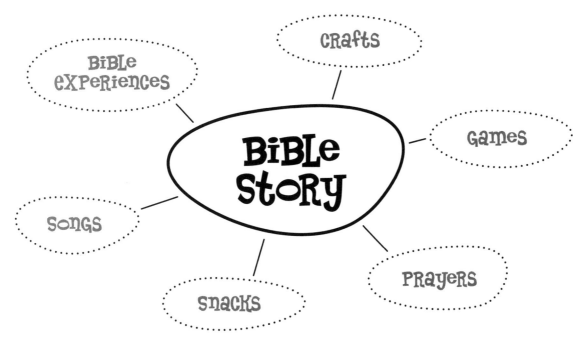

Every Humongous Bible story has some snack activities. Keep this tip in mind when using food with your preschoolers.

Be aware that some children have food allergies that can be dangerous. Know your children, and consult with parents about allergies their children may have. Also, be sure to read food labels carefully, as hidden ingredients can cause allergy-related problems.

So let the adventure begin for you and your preschoolers! Use these humongous Bible ideas to help your preschoolers grow closer to Jesus in humongous ways!

GOD MADE THE WORLD

Bible Basis:

Genesis 1:1-31

Supplies:

Bible, blank poster board, one piece of yellow paper, one piece of black paper, glue sticks, 5-10 cotton balls, 3-4 silk flowers, star stickers, markers, animal and people stickers

Have the children form a circle and sit down. Place the blank poster board on the floor in the center of the circle. Set the "creation items" you gathered before class on the floor beside you. Open your Bible to Genesis 1, and show the children the words.

Say ▶ **Today's Bible story teaches us that God made everything.**

"In the beginning God created the heavens and the earth." He didn't do it all at once. He took seven days to create the world. We are going to sing about what God created each day. "Sing" the following phrases as you would say the ditty "A shave and a haircut: two bits."

Sing ▶ **God created day and night: day one.** *(Hold up one finger.)*

Day 1

Say ▶ **On the first day, "God said, 'Let there be light,' and there was light… Then he separated the light from the darkness. God called the light 'day,' and the darkness 'night.' " God created light.** Point to the poster, and have one child glue the yellow piece of paper to the poster and another child glue the black piece of paper to the poster. **Let's sing this together.**

Sing ▶ **God created day and night: day one.** *(Hold up one finger.)*

Day 2

Say ▶ **On the second day, God said there should be a big space between the waters below and the water above, and it was so. God called the big space "sky."** Point to the poster, and have one child glue the cotton ball clouds to the poster. **Let's sing that together.**

Sing ▶ **God created the sky: day two.** *(Hold up two fingers.)*

Day 3

Say ▸ On the third day, God said that the water on the earth should be gathered to one place so that dry ground could appear. "And that is what happened. God called the dry ground 'land,' and the waters 'seas.'" Then God put trees, plants, and flowers on the land to grow. **God made land, water, and plants.** Point to the poster, and have several children glue the silk flowers to the poster. **Let's try to sing all that together.**

Sing ▸ **God created land, water, and plants: day three.** *(Hold up three fingers.)*

Day 4

Say ▸ God said, "Let great lights appear in the sky to separate the day from the night…Let these lights in the sky shine down on the earth." **God made the sun, moon, and stars.** Point to the poster, and have children place the star stickers on the poster. **Let's sing together.**

Sing ▸ **God created the sun, moon, and stars: day four.** *(Hold up four fingers.)*

Say ▸ **Let's find out what God created on day five.**

Day 5

Say ▸ God said that the oceans should be filled with fish and that other creatures and birds should fly across the sky. **So God created all kinds of fish and birds.** Point to the poster, and encourage a few children to use markers to draw simple fish or birds on the poster. **Let's sing together.**

Sing ▸ **God created fish and birds: day five.** *(Hold up five fingers.)*

Say ▸ **God made everything in just the right order. Our God loves us. Let's find out what God created on day six.**

Day 6

Say ▸ God said animals should fill the land. And it happened. God made wild animals, farm animals, and animals that crawl along the ground. And all the animals made God happy. Then God said that he would make a man. Then he made a woman to be the man's helper. And God was very happy. **God created animals and people.**

Point to the poster, and have each child put an animal or person sticker on the poster. **Let's sing together.**

sing ➤ **God created animals and people: day six.** *(Hold up six fingers.)*

Day 7

say ➤ **On day seven, God rested and enjoyed what he had made. He didn't rest because he was tired but because he was finished. God had created everything. One last time, let's sing.**

sing ➤ **God created the world in seven days.** *(Hold up seven fingers.)*

ask ➤ • **What are some things God created?**

say ➤ **In the beginning, God made everything. Jesus was with God in the beginning when God created everything. We can get to know Jesus better by spending time outside and by enjoying the things God made.**

BiBLe eXPeRienCes

Creation Walk

Supplies: sidewalk chalk

Take your class outdoors to a sidewalk or paved area. Review the days of creation, and then have each child use sidewalk chalk to draw a large circle. Beginning with the first day of creation, assign one or two children to each day. Encourage kids to draw a picture in their circle of the work God did on that day of creation. If your class is large and space is limited, draw the largest circle possible, then have kids gather around the circle and add their favorite part of God's creation.

Signs of the Seasons

Supplies: seasonal dress-up clothes

Bring in seasonal dress-up clothes for children to try on. Include items such as sunglasses, raincoats, umbrellas, winter coats and hats, mittens, and boots. As children try on the clothes, have them tell you what they like about each season and how they might need to dress for that time of year. Remind children that God made our world and God made each season different from the others.

Let There Be Light

Supplies: Bible, a sheet of black construction paper for each child, glow-in-the-dark star stickers

Before this activity, remove the glow-in-the-dark star stickers from their package. Set them in a place where they have direct exposure to a light source such as a window or lamp. This allows the stickers to absorb plenty of light so they'll glow brightly.

Hold up a sheet of black paper.

say **Before God made our world, everything was completely dark, like this paper. There was nothing in the world—not a sun or a moon or stars. Let's close our eyes to see what that might have been like.**

Close your eyes, and direct the children to do the same. Tell children to keep their eyes closed until you say to open them. You might suggest that they put their hands over their eyes to make it "extra" dark. While their eyes are still closed,

ask • **What do you see?**

• **What would it be like if our world was like this all the time?**

say **In the Bible, the first thing God said was "Let there be light." And the world became bright! Let's call out together, "Let there be light!" just as God did. Then we'll open our eyes and see what happens.**

Have the children call out with you, "Let there be light!" When they've opened their eyes,

ask • **Now what do you see?**

say **Giving light to the whole world is something only God can do! Only God can make light as bright as the sun or as pretty as the stars.**

Give each child a sheet of black construction paper.

say **Let's add something special to our dark pieces of paper to remember that when God made our world, God gave us light, too. You may each put one of these star stickers on your paper. When you place your sticker on your paper, say, "Thank you, God, for making our world."**

Distribute the glow-in-the-dark star stickers, and let children place stickers on their papers as they say, "Thank you, God, for making our world." When everyone has finished, **say** **Now turn your paper over so you can't see your star. When I turn off the light, let's all call out, "Let there be light!" just as God did. Then we'll turn our papers over again, and we'll see a big surprise!**

Be sure the children have turned their papers star-side down before you turn off the lights. Then, when they've turned their papers back over to show their stars, **say** > **Wow! Our papers look brighter now! Because God made light, our world looks brighter, too.**

Encourage the children to place their starry pictures next to their beds at home so they'll remember God's gift of light even when it's dark outside.

Open your Bible to Genesis 1:1, and show children the verse.

say > **The Bible tells us that God made the world. I'm glad God put lights in the sky so we could see all the wonderful things he has made.**

CRafts

Fill the World

Supplies: newsprint, tempera paint, plastic spoons, bowls, cotton balls, seeds, paint shirts, tape, newspaper or vinyl tablecloth

Tape several large sheets of newsprint together, and lay them on a table. To protect the floor, cover it with newspapers or a vinyl tablecloth. Set out bowls of blue, yellow, green, and brown tempera paint, and have children put on paint shirts.

Gather children around the table. If you have more than 10 children in your class, you may want to set up two tables and make two murals.

say > **This paper is empty, just as our world was empty before God started creating things to live in it. Let's fill up this paper with the creations that God made. We're going to make lots of things to go on our picture, and everyone will get a turn to help.**

ask > **• What did God make for us to walk on?**

say > **God made the ground. Let's put some dirt in our picture. I'll pass out spoons to paint with, and then I'll ask three people to paint some dirt at the bottom of our picture.**

Give plastic spoons to three children, and show them how to use the backs of the spoons to paint the brown paint onto the newsprint. Have children set their spoons in the brown paint bowl when they're through.

ask > **• What grows in the ground?**

say > **God made plants to grow in the ground. Plants start out as little seeds. [Name] and [name], will you sprinkle some seeds on our ground?**

Give each of the two children a spoonful of seeds. Have them start at opposite ends of the newsprint and sprinkle their seeds in the "dirt."

ask • What kinds of plants should we put in our picture?

say **God made lots of different kinds of plants. He made trees, bushes, flowers, and grass. Let's put some grass in our picture first. I need three grass painters.** Give spoons to three children, and have them paint grass above the dirt. Then invite other children to add green bushes, brown tree trunks, green treetops, and blue or yellow flowers. Make sure each child gets a turn to paint. Have children return their spoons to the appropriate paint bowls when they're through.

What a beautiful picture of God's world! What should go at the top of our picture? (Sky; clouds; sun.) **God made the sun and put it up in the sky. Let's put a sky and a sun in our picture.** Choose two children to paint a blue sky and one child to paint a yellow sun. Distribute cotton balls, and let children stick "clouds" in the sky, then let all the children paint several raindrops.

ask • What else did God make that's missing in our picture?

say **God made our world and everything in it.** Leave the creation mural on the table for about an hour to dry. When the paint is no longer wet, you can hang it up in your classroom to remind children of God's creations.

Swirling Colors

Supplies: paint smocks, blank paper, milk, eyedropper, green and blue food coloring, dish soap, paper towels, watercolor paints, markers

Have the children put on paint smocks. Distribute a blank paper to each child, and have kids write their names on their papers. Ask a child to help you demonstrate on one of the papers what it might have looked like as God created the earth. Use the eyedropper to slowly make a 2- to 2½-inch puddle of milk on the center of the page (the milk will stay in a puddle without running if the surface is flat). Place one drop of green food coloring and one drop of blue food coloring about ¾-inch apart on the puddle of milk. Then have the child carefully put a single drop of dishwashing liquid between the drops of food coloring. Let everyone watch the swirling colors! Then have the child lay folded paper towels on the page to absorb the liquid. A small amount of the swirled design will remain on the page. Let the other children try the experiment on their pages, then have them use watercolors to finish creating their colorful worlds.

ask • What did you like most about making your colorful page?

• What's one thing that God created that you're thankful for? Why?

• How can we thank God for creating so many wonderful things?

say **God made everything in the heavens and on the beautiful earth. Let's remember to pray, sing, worship, and thank God for all of the good things he has made.**

PRAYERS

Wonderful Creation Prayer

Supplies: none

Ask the kids each to think of one thing from creation that they want to praise God for, then let the kids try to pantomime their ideas. For example, a child might get down on all fours and pretend to be a puppy or wiggle his or her fingers as the stars in the sky. Then say the following prayer, and have kids do their actions when indicated.

> **Dear God,**
>
> **We praise you for...** (Go around the circle and have the kids each pantomime their praise.)
>
> **We thank you, God, for everything you've made.**
>
> **In Jesus' name, amen.**

Action Prayer

Form a circle, and have the children sit down.

say ▸ **We've learned that God made everything. Let's thank God for some of those things. Pray the words after me while we do the motions together.**

Lord, we thank you for the flowers. *(Hold up fingers and wiggle them.)*

Lord, we thank you for the trees. *(Make a circle overhead with your arms.)*

Lord, we thank you for spring showers *(raise fingers high, and wiggle them as you lower them),*

And we thank you for the bees. *(Touch middle finger to thumb on each hand. Make small, fluttering circular motions in the air.)*

Lord, we thank you for the food we eat. *(Lift closed hand to mouth as if eating with a spoon.)*

Lord, we thank you for birds so sweet. *(Hook thumbs together, and wiggle fingers while moving hands around.)*

Lord, we thank you for the cows that moo *(stretch neck as you say the "moo" sound),*

And we thank you for your love so true. *(Cover heart with hands.)*

In Jesus' name, amen.

snacks

A Yummy Creation

Supplies: sandwich cookies, resealable sandwich bags, chocolate pudding, gummy worms, spoons, cups

Before beginning, have kids wash their hands. Distribute the snack supplies to the children. Have kids use their fists to crush their sandwich cookies inside the resealable bags. Fill 5-ounce cups about two-thirds full with chocolate pudding. Let kids mix their cookie crumbs and gummy worms into the pudding with their spoons. Choose a child to thank God for providing the snack. As children eat their snacks, remind them that God loves them even more than God loves the little animals.

ask
- **What do you like best in your snack creation?**
- **What do you like best in God's creation?**

say **Everything God made is wonderful! It's fun to think about the things in creation that we like and to thank God for those things. God made everything, and everything God made is good.**

songs

God Made the World

Supplies: none

Have children join you as you sing "God Made the World" (adapted from Genesis 1:1) to the tune of "The Farmer in the Dell."

> **God made the world.**
> **Oh, God made the world.**
> **We thank him for creating it.**
> **God made the world!**
>
> **God made the light.**
> **Oh, God made the light.**
> **We thank him for creating it.**
> **God made the light!**
>
> **God made you and me.**
> **Oh, God made you and me.**
> **We thank him for creating us.**
> **God made you and me!**

Everything Was Good

Supplies: none

Lead children in singing "Everything Was Good" to the tune of "Old MacDonald Had a Farm."

Long ago God made the world,
And everything was good.
God made light and day and night,
And everything was good.
Growing plants,
Stars, moon, sun—
Playing in God's world is fun!
Long ago God made the world,
And everything was good.

Long ago God made the world,
And everything was good.
Animals and people, too.
And everything was good.
God made [name]**.**
God made [name]**.**
God made [name] **and** [name] **and** [name]**.**
Long ago God made the world,
And everything was good.

God Made People

Bible Basis:

 Genesis 1:26-31; 2:4-25

Supplies:

Bible, 2 sheets of blank poster board, clay, bone-shaped dog biscuit, paper plates

Open your Bible to Genesis 2, and show children the words.

say > **Today's Bible story tells us that God made us. Let's find out what it was like when God made the first people—Adam and Eve.**

People today are born as tiny babies, but do you know how Adam was born? Not as a tiny baby…God made Adam from the dust of the ground! Maybe from something a little like this. Show children the clay. Give each child a handful of clay on a paper plate, and let kids explore the texture.

God made Adam first. What part of Adam do you think God started with? Allow the children to guess different body parts, and assign each child to sculpt a different part with his or her clay. Make sure that the arms, legs, torso, and head are represented. Have kids put together the pieces of clay on one of the sheets of poster board to form Adam's body. As children work, continue with the story.

God made each part of Adam so that all the parts worked together. God made Adam's eyes and nose, arms and legs, and hands and feet. God gave Adam a heart to pump blood and a brain to think with. God made Adam perfectly. God made Adam, and God made us! Help the children finish making the Adam figure.

After God created Adam, the Bible says that God breathed life into Adam. We worked very hard to form this clay body, but we can't breathe life into him, can we? Only God can give life! Lay out the second sheet of poster board, and give each child another handful of clay.

Later, God decided that Adam needed a helper. So God made Adam fall asleep. Have kids snore loudly as they pretend to sleep. **Then God took a rib from Adam's side and made another person, Eve, to be a friend to Adam.** Hold up a bone-shaped dog biscuit. **We'll pretend that this is Adam's rib.**

God made a woman—Eve—out of Adam's rib. Let's put clay around this rib to make a figure of Eve. Lay the biscuit on the second sheet of poster board, and let kids make a torso to cover it. Tell the kids to shape arms, legs, and a head, and then let them form a figure of Eve.

When God finished making the woman, he brought her to Adam. Adam and Eve lived in a beautiful garden called the Garden of Eden! Put the sheets of poster board next to each other.

ask • **Why do you think God made both Adam and Eve?**

• **Why do you think God made us?**

• **What do you like best about the way God made you?**

say **God made Adam and Eve, and God made us! God made each one of you in awesome ways! You can breathe, eat, sleep, move, see, hear, smell, taste, and feel things!**

BiBLe eXPeRieNceS

Beating Hearts

Supplies: stethoscope

Let kids each listen to their heartbeats through a stethoscope. Remind children that God breathed life into Adam and Adam's heart began to beat just like theirs are beating now. Tell kids that a beating heart means we are alive and only God can give life.

Playful People

Supplies: modeling dough

Set out modeling dough, and help children make a variety of people figures. Encourage them to identify the people they've made. For example, they might make a small person to represent a younger sibling and a larger person to represent a parent or other adult. As children work, tell them that today's Bible story is about the first people God made. Remind them that God made our world and you and me.

CRAFTS

Mirror, Mirror

Supplies: blank paper, markers, paint smocks, finger paints, mirrors

Distribute paper, and have the kids write their names on their papers. Let the children put on paint smocks or old shirts, and have the kids look at their faces in the mirrors. Instruct the children each to use the finger paints to paint on the mirror the reflection they see, including their eyes, nose, mouth, and other features. After the kids have painted their faces on the mirror, help them gently press blank pieces of paper against the mirror and then lift the pages to reveal pictures of themselves—unique, special children who were made by God.

ask
- **What's special about your face?**
- **Why do you think God made so many different, wonderful people in the world?**

say **God made you and me. Each of us is beautiful and precious to God. God made us so we can love and praise him forever.**

Have the kids show each other their mirror images. Ask each child to complete this sentence: "I praise God for how he made…" Children might finish the sentence by saying something like "my brown eyes so I can see." Praise God for how he made us!

Unique Prints

Supplies: several magnifying glasses, an ink pad, wet wipes, and plain white index cards

Let children take turns making their fingerprints on index cards and then looking at their prints closely through a magnifying glass. Help children compare fingerprints with one another and look for the similarities and differences in each one. Tell kids that today they will learn that God made each person special and unique in many ways.

One, Two, Many People

Supplies: 2 plastic foam cups per student, 1 small "baby" cup per student, markers

say **In our Bible story today, we learned that God made Adam and Eve, the first people. We're going to make Adam and Eve figures so we can remember that God made Adam and Eve—and all of us.**

Give each child two foam cups. Have each child turn the cups upside down and then use markers to draw Adam on the first cup.

say ▶ **Adam was very lonely without a helper. Let's make Eve so Adam has someone to talk to and play with in the Garden of Eden.**

Direct children to each use markers to draw Eve on the second cup. Allow children to play with their "dolls," making the cups "walk" along the table and talk to each other.

ask ▶ • **Why do you think God made Adam and Eve?**

Bring out a sample of nesting dolls with Adam on top, Eve underneath, and a small paper cup on the bottom. Show them to the children as you speak.

say ▶ **God made Adam.** Point to the top doll. **Then God made Eve from Adam.** Pull up the first cup to show Eve underneath. **Then God made all of us from Adam and Eve.** Pull up the second cup to show the baby cup underneath. Give each child a baby cup, and encourage kids to take home the nesting dolls and use them to tell their families the story of how God made Adam, Eve, and everyone in the world.

Games

Beautiful Reflections

Supplies: none

say ▶ **God made us alike in many ways. He gave us hands, feet, eyes, ears, and many other parts. Some parts, like our heart and our brain, are inside our bodies. We can't see those parts, but we know they are there. Other parts are on the outside, and we can see them when we look in a mirror. Whenever we do, we should thank God for the wonderful way he made us. Let's pretend to be mirrors and thank God for making us.**

Let the kids stand face to face with another child. Have one child in each pair imitate the movements of his or her partner. Encourage the other partner to listen to your directions and follow the actions you suggest. Go through the actions once, and then have kids switch roles.

say ▶ **God made my arms to reach up high.**

God made my hands to clap.

My feet can step up and down…and sometimes I like to run.

I like to button my shirt and put on a hat.

I like to peel a banana and eat it all up.

My head can go up and down and back and forth.

I can fold my hands and pray.

ask • What do you like the most about yourself?

• How can you thank God for making you that way?

say God made us, and God loves us. We can thank God for the special way that he made each of us by using our bodies to serve him and to worship him.

We're Special

Supplies: none

say God made our world and each person here, so each one of you is special! That means God made you different from everyone else in the whole wide world and loves you very much. Let's play a game to help us remember that.

I'm going to give you some directions. If you hear me say, "If you're special" before the directions, do what I say. For example, I might say, "If you're special, stand up."

Have children stand up.

say You'll have to listen carefully. Don't follow my directions unless you hear me say, "If you're special."

Read the following instructions, one at a time. Each time you say, "If you're special," pause for children to complete their actions. As you speak, put extra emphasis on "If you're special" to make sure children hear and follow the directions.

• If you're special, hug yourself.

• If you're special, shake a friend's hand.

• If you're a mouse, crawl on the floor.

• If you're strong, make a fist.

• If you're special, pat someone on the back.

• If you're special, hug someone.

• If you're in our class, sit down.

• If you're special, jump up and shout, "I'm special!" then sit down.

PRAYERS

"You Made Me" Prayer

Supplies: none

Teach the children this action prayer. Say each line and do the action, then have the kids repeat after you.

> **Dear God** (fold hands in prayer),
> **You made my toes to tap.** (Tap toes.)
> **You made my hands to clap.** (Clap hands.)
> **You made my body to sway.** (Sway from side to side.)
> **You made my voice to pray.** (Place hands by mouth.)
> **And I thank you, God** (raise arms high),
> **That I am wonderfully made.** (Hug self.)
> **In Jesus' name, amen.**

SNACKS

Cookie-People Snack

Supplies: vanilla wafers, frosting, craft sticks, chocolate chips, thin licorice, M&M'S candies

Before class, create some person-shaped cookies with the supplies. At snack time, set out the sample cookies that you prepared before class. Encourage kids to use the craft sticks to spread the frosting onto the cookies. Help children say a prayer of thanks that God made their bodies and provided their snack today. Then let kids enjoy their treat!

ask • Why do you think God made our arms? What about our legs?

• How can you thank God for the wonderful way he made you?

say God made us so we can do wonderful things like singing and running and giving people hugs. God made us special!

God Made Us!

Supplies: Fruit by the Foot, wax paper, three types of small round cookies

Ask the children to wash their hands. Then give each child one of each of the three different cookies, a 15-inch length of wax paper, and three 12-inch pieces of Fruit by the Foot. Show the kids how to tear the pieces of fruit to make three stick figure bodies: Adam, Eve, and themselves. Let the children place the figures on wax paper, then place a different kind of round cookie at the top of each stick figure as the head.

After the children have made the figures, teach the kids this rhyme.

 God made Adam. *(Point to one figure.)*

God made Eve. *(Point to the second figure.)*

And then one day, God made me! *(Point to the third figure.)*

Ask a child to pray, then let everyone eat and enjoy the snacks. Provide resealable plastic bags so that the children can take home any leftover snacks.

ask • **How many people do you think there are in the world?**

• **Why do you think God made all those people?**

say **God made all the people in the world! And God loves all those people. God wants us to love each other and be happy together.**

Songs

"Thank You" Rhyme

Supplies: none

 Thank you, God,

For feet that run *(run in place)*

And hop and jump *(hop on one foot and then both)*

And have such fun. *(Keep hopping.)*

Thank you, God,

For hands that clap *(clap hands)*

And wiggle and wave *(wiggle fingers and wave hands)*

And pet a cat. *(Pet the back of your fist as if it's a cat.)*

Thank you, God,

For making me *(point both thumbs at yourself)*

And moms and dads *(hold up one index finger and then the other)*

And friends to see. *(Hold up both hands and wiggle all your fingers.)*

We love you and praise you *(cross arms over heart and then raise them with palms up)*

And shout out your name. *(Cup hands around mouth and shout the last two lines.)*

Our God is forever

And ever the same!

God Made You, God Made Me

Supplies: none

Lead children in singing "God Made You, God Made Me" to the tune of "This Old Man." As you sing, join hands and walk around together.

God made you; God made me.
God made each one differently,
But we're all part of one big family.
God made each one differently.

God made you; God made me.
God made everyone we see,
But we're all part of one big family.
God made everyone we see.

NoaH and tHe arK

Bible Basis:

Genesis 6:5–8:13

Supplies:

Bible, paper plates, crayons or markers, poster board, building blocks, sunflower seeds, small plastic animals or animal stickers, one piece of brown construction paper, spray bottles filled with water

Choose a child to be Noah. Have the other children form groups to play the following parts: men, women, pigs, hens, snakes, mice, and owls. Give each child a paper plate, and have the kids draw and color simple masks to represent their characters while you continue with the lesson. Open your Bible to Genesis 6, and show children the words.

say ▶ **Today's Bible story tells us that God wants us to obey. People fought and thought mean things about each other. But God wanted people to obey him. Let's use our masks during the story.**

Have the groups line up with their masks in this order: men, women, pigs, hens, snakes, mice, owls, and "Noah." Tell the kids that when you ask a question in the story, the children representing each character will hold their masks in front of their faces and say their lines. The children will all say "Not I," except Noah, who will say, "I will—God wants me to obey."

say ▶ **As I was saying, back in Noah's day, people were bad. God asked, "Who will say they're sorry and be kind?"**

"Not I," shouted the men.

"Not I," yelled the women.

"Not I," grunted the pigs.

"Not I," clucked the hens.

"Not I," hissed the snakes.

"Not I," squeaked the mice.

"Not I," hooted the owls.

"I will—God wants me to obey," said Noah.

say ▶ **God was sad. He said, "I'll send a flood of water because I'm sad that people are so mean. But I'm happy that Noah obeys me. I want a huge boat to be built so that Noah, his family, and some animals will live. Who will help me build the ark?"** Have the kids say their lines. **So Noah obeyed God and built the ark. Noah cut and sawed and sanded and pounded until, finally, the ark was done.** Have Noah build a small ark with building blocks on top of poster board. **God asked, "Who will help load food onto the ark for the animals?"**

Have the kids say their lines.

say ▶ **Noah loaded food onto the ark.** Have Noah put sunflower seeds or another type of grain inside the ark. **Then God sent the animals, two of each. Onto the ark galloped horses and zebras. Onto the ark pounded elephants and hippos.** Encourage kids to put small plastic animals into the ark or they can put stickers on the poster board. **Finally this squeaking, squawking zoo was ready to go. When Noah and his family were safely inside the ark, God shut the door.** Put a piece of brown construction paper over the top of the block ark. **It started to rain and rain and rain.** Let kids squirt water from a water bottle over the ark. **I wonder who wanted to be on the ark now.** Have kids put their masks back on and say these new lines:

"I wish I was," shouted the men.

"I wish I was," yelled the women.

"I wish I was," grunted the pigs.

"I wish I was," clucked the hens.

"I wish I was," hissed the snakes.

"I wish I was," squeaked the mice.

"I wish I was," hooted the owls.

"I was on the ark—I obeyed God," said Noah.

ask ▶ • **How did Noah obey God?**

• **How do you obey God?**

• **Why does God want us to obey him?**

say ▶ **Noah obeyed God, and everyone on the ark was safe from the flood. And when the rain stopped, God sent a beautiful rainbow! The rainbow showed God's promise to never flood the whole earth again. It was a promise of God's love for us.**

When we obey God, we show God that we love him, too. Let's be like Noah and obey God in all we say and do.

When Jesus was on earth, he always obeyed God and did what God wanted him to do. We can learn from Jesus and follow his example. We can also ask Jesus to help us obey God. Jesus obeyed God every day, so he can help us to obey God, too. God wants us to obey!

BiBLe eXPeRieNceS

Guess the Animal

Supplies: none

Gather children in a circle, and tell them they will have to listen very carefully. Have kids take turns making several different animal sounds, and have everyone else try to guess which animal is making each sound. Remind the children that even the animals obeyed God and went into the ark.

ask ▸ • **What do you think it was like on the ark with all those animals?**

• **How can you obey God?**

say ▸ **God wants us to obey. God knows what's best for us, and when we obey God, we are doing the right thing. We can obey God, just as Noah obeyed God.**

Colorful Promise

Supplies: circles, squares, and triangles (approximately 4 inches wide) cut from a variety of colored cellophane—use primary colors: red, yellow, and blue, as well as other colors if you choose; flashlights

Encourage children to hold up the shapes and shine flashlights through the cellophane. Encourage children to experiment with different amounts of light and overlapping colors. Can they guess the results when different colors overlap? Tell children that when it stopped raining and the flood waters went away, God made a rainbow of many bright colors to show his love.

Obedience Wears Many Hats

Supplies: strips of paper; paper clips; stapler; small pieces of paper in the following colors: red, yellow, green, blue; tape

say ▸ **Noah was good at obeying God. He thought about God and loved God. You can think about God and love God, too. Let's make hats to remind us of our story!**

Help the children measure the strips around their heads, tilting them up slightly at the forehead. Use paper clips to secure the strips at the right length, then take the strips off their heads without moving the paper clips. Staple the headbands in the back, and take off paper clips.

say ▸ **Noah had some neat adventures by trying out new jobs that God gave him. God gave Noah special plans to follow for building the ark. Noah had never done that before, but he still obeyed.** Hold up the red paper. **Noah had to be just like an engineer and draw out the special plans for the ark. Let's put a piece of red on the front of our headbands and pretend that we are wearing a red engineer hat for our new job.** Staple the red paper onto the hats.

Next, God told Noah to build the ark. Noah had never built an ark before, but he still obeyed. Let's put yellow on our bands like a yellow construction hat for Noah's new building job. Have children place the yellow paper beside, or just overlapping, the red paper, and staple it in place.

Then God told Noah to put wild animals in the ark. Noah had never taken care of wild animals before, but he still obeyed. Let's put a green piece on our bands like a park ranger's or zookeeper's hat. Have children place the green paper beside, or just overlapping, the yellow paper, and staple it in place.

Finally, God told Noah to get in the ark and sail it. Noah had never sailed an ark before, but he still obeyed. Let's put a blue piece on our band like a sailor's hat. Have children place the blue paper beside, or just overlapping, the green paper, and staple it in place.

Make sure each child puts the papers close together so you can reinforce them with a line of tape at the top. Bend each paper slightly to look like the bill of a visor. Cut any excess paper, then have everyone try on these special "job" hats. Trim around the corners of the bill if needed.

ask ▸ • **Which of Noah's jobs would you like best? Why?**

• **How can you obey God just as Noah did?**

say ▸ **God wants us to obey. God has some special jobs for us, just as God had some special and exciting jobs for Noah. God loves us. He will help us have wonderful adventures and do many different and exciting jobs for him!**

CRAFTS

Thumbprint Arks

Supplies: paper plates cut into the shape of arks, crayons (brown, black, white), washable stamp pads, pens, wet wipes

Give children each one of the paper plate arks and have them write their names on the back. Distribute brown crayons for children to color their arks. Encourage kids to use white or black crayons to draw windows in the top part of the ark. Provide a washable stamp pad for every three children. Show children how to press both of their thumbs onto the stamp pad and then make thumbprints close together on the ark. Encourage kids to use pens to add details to turn the thumbprints into pairs of bugs, birds, animals, or people. Have wet wipes nearby for children to clean their fingers.

say God planned to bless Noah and his family by saving them from the flood. Noah obeyed God and built the ark. God wants us to obey by trusting in Jesus. When we trust in Jesus, he helps us obey and do things God's way.

ask • When we disobey, what should we do?

• Who can help us obey?

• What are some good things that come from trusting in Jesus?

say God loves us even when we disobey. God promises to forgive us when we trust in Jesus. God wants us to obey by trusting Jesus, who helps us live the way God wants us to.

Noah's Ark

Supplies: blank paper with ark shape drawn on it, magazine pictures of animals (already cut out), shredded wheat cereal, glue

Set out the magazine pictures of animals you cut out before class, shredded wheat cereal (for the animals' food), and glue. Remind kids that it's important to follow directions, just as Noah followed God's directions when he built the ark.

say God wants us to obey.

Explain to the children that they should glue the animal pictures onto their arks. Then have children glue on the animals' food.

ask • How did you obey my directions in this activity?

• How can you obey God?

say We can obey God by following God's directions, just as Noah did. God gives us his directions through the Bible, through our parents, and through teachers. God wants us to obey.

3-D Rainbows

Supplies: blank paper with an ark drawn on it (make one and copy the others for the students), crayons, cotton balls, glue, gummy animals

Have children wash their hands in case they want to snack on some of the gummy animals. Then distribute the blank "ark" pages, and have kids write their names on their papers. Ask kids to draw a rainbow over their ark. Encourage children to glue cotton balls as clouds around the rainbow. Have kids form pairs, and let them use gummy animals as they tell their partners the story of Noah's ark.

ask • **What did God put in the sky as a promise? Why?**

• **What will you remember the next time you see a rainbow?**

say **God sent a rainbow to Noah and promised that he would never send another flood to cover the whole earth. The next time you see a rainbow, remember that God keeps all his promises.**

PRayeRS

"Help Me to Obey" Prayer

Supplies: none

Ask the kids to obey you by repeating your words and actions in this prayer.

> **Dear God** (fold hands in prayer),
> **Help me always obey you.** (Raise hands high.)
> **I pray that you'll be pleased.** (Nod head.)
> **In Jesus' name, amen.** (Fold hands in prayer.)

snacks

Edible Arks

Supplies: animal crackers, pretzel sticks, bowls, paper plates

Have children wash their hands before the snack. Place animal crackers and pretzel sticks in bowls within kids' reach. Encourage children to use the pretzels to outline an ark on a paper plate and make paths leading to the ark.

Encourage kids to identify the animal crackers and try to make pairs of each animal. Then have kids pretend to march the animals along the paths to the pretzel ark. As they play and snack, encourage children to talk about each animal and all the special things that animal does.

ask
- **What is your favorite animal that God made? Why?**
- **How can we take good care of the animals and the world God made?**

say
God made everything very good. God showed his love by caring for Noah and his family. Noah showed his love by obeying God and building the ark. God wants us to obey, too! If we have pets, we can obey by taking good care of them. We care for God's world when we pick up trash. We can remember to thank God for the wonderful animals he created.

Rainbow Snacks

Supplies: bowls of 1-inch gelatin squares of different colors, paper plates, wet wipes

Have children wash their hands before eating their snack. Place bowls of gelatin squares within kids' reach, and give each child a paper plate. Let each child take four or five squares of each color. Encourage kids to use the squares to make rainbow designs on their plates. Move through the room affirming kids' designs. Invite one child to pray and thank God for the snacks and for his wonderful rainbow promise. Encourage children to enjoy the colorful snacks. When children have finished eating, use wet wipes to clean any sticky hands.

ask
- **When have you seen a real rainbow?**
- **What can we remember each time we see a rainbow?**
- **What are some of God's promises? Which is your favorite?**

say
God made a rainbow as a promise that he would never again destroy the earth with a flood. Noah saw the rainbow and trusted God to keep his promise. We can trust God, too. He will always love and care for us. When we see a rainbow, we can remember that God keeps all his promises.

Arky, Arky

Supplies: none

Hold hands in a circle, and swing hands back and forth.

say ▶ **Let's sing a song about the Bible story.** Encourage the kids to sing the words and do the actions with you.

The Lord told Noah, there's gonna be a floody, floody. *(Hold arms up, then wiggle fingers to make "rain.")*
Lord told Noah there's gonna be a floody, floody.
Get those animals out of the muddy, muddy, children of the Lord. *(Shake index finger.)*

The Lord told Noah to build him an arky, arky. *(Point up on "Lord," then pound on palm with fist.)*
Lord told Noah to build him an arky, arky.
Build it out of gopher barky, barky, children of the Lord. *(Pretend to hammer.)*

The animals, the animals, they came in by twosies, twosies. *(Hold up two fingers and march to the beat.)*
Animals, the animals, they came in by twosies, twosies.
Elephants and kangaroosies, 'roosies, children of the Lord. *(Swing arms like an elephant's trunk, then hop like a kangaroo.)*

It rained and poured for 40 daysies, daysies. *(Wiggle fingers to make "rain.")*
Rained and poured for 40 daysies, daysies.
Almost drove those animals crazies, crazies, children of the Lord. *(Put hands on either side of your face, open eyes wide.)*

The sun came up and dried up the landy, landy. *(Make a big circle with arms.)*
Look, there's the sun—it dried up the landy, landy.
Everything was fine and dandy, dandy, children of the Lord. *(Hold out arms and twirl in a circle.)*

So rise and shine and give God the glory, glory. *(Raise arms, and spread fingers wide like sunshine.)*
Rise and shine and give God the glory, glory.
Rise and shine and give God the glory, glory, children of the Lord.

A Rainbow of Color

Supplies: colorful streamers

Give each child two or three streamers of different colors. Have the children listen to you sing "The Lord Will Keep His Promises," which is sung to the tune of "The Muffin Man." Encourage kids to walk or skip around in a circle, waving their streamers from side to side to the music. During the last line of each verse, "God never tells a lie," have the children hold the streamers high above their heads as they spin around.

SING ▶ The Lord will keep his promises, promises, promises.
The Lord will keep his promises.
God never tells a lie.

Noah obeyed and built the ark, built the ark, built the ark.
Noah obeyed and built the ark.
God never tells a lie.

Animals on the ark came two by two, two by two, two by two.
Animals on the ark came two by two.
God never tells a lie.

God shut the door when the rain came down, rain came down, rain came down.
God shut the door when the rain came down.
God never tells a lie.

It rained and poured for 40 days, 40 days, 40 days.
It rained and poured for 40 days.
God never tells a lie.

The boat hit land when the water dried, water dried, water dried.
The boat hit land when the water dried.
God never tells a lie.

The Lord will keep his promises, promises, promises.
The Lord will keep his promises.
God never tells a lie.

Say ▶ We can always trust God to keep his promises! God keeps all his promises.

JOSEPH TeLLS HiS DReams

Bible Basis:

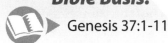 Genesis 37:1-11

Supplies:

Bible, large blank paper for a mural taped to the wall, crayons

Open your Bible to Genesis 37, and show children the words.

say ▸ **Today's Bible story tells us that families need to show God's love. We're going to learn about a family that didn't always show God's love. While we learn about what happened to Joseph and his family, we're going to make a big picture on this paper** (point to the paper on the wall) **to help us remember that families need to show God's love.**

Maybe some of you have teenage baby sitters. Well, Joseph was a teenager when this story happened. He had 11 brothers! Can you believe that? What a lot of boys in a family!

ask ▸ • **How many brothers or sisters do you have?**

Invite children to come up to the mural and make simple stick-figure people to represent each of the brothers. Remind children to keep their drawings about an inch away from the edges of the paper so their crayons don't slip and mark the wall.

say ▸ **One day, Joseph and his brothers were taking care of their father's sheep.**

ask ▸ • **What things do you do for your parents that show you love them?**

say ▸ **Families need to show God's love. We can show God's love to our parents by obeying them and doing our chores without whining or complaining, and we can be kind to our brothers and sisters.**

The Bible tells us that the brothers were taking care of the sheep. Close your eyes, and try to picture a big grassy field with sheep and all those brothers. I'm sure the boys had to work together to take care of that many sheep. Let's draw some grass and sheep on our mural. Invite other children to add grass and lots of sheep to the mural.

Maybe the brothers shared food and water or took turns caring for hurt sheep.

ask ▸ • **How do you show God's love to your family?**

say ▸ We can show God's love to our families by being kind, sharing our things, or helping with chores. Families need to show God's love.

The Bible tells us that one day Joseph brought a bad report to his father about his brothers. We might say that he tattled on his brothers.

ask ▸ · What do you think Joseph might have told his father?

say ▸ Whatever happened, it sounds like the brothers were not showing God's love to one another. I'm sure the brothers were really angry with Joseph for tattling.

But Joseph was his father's favorite son. This made the brothers even angrier. To show Joseph how much he loved him, Joseph's father had a special coat made for him. It was a really beautiful coat with lots of bright colors on it.

Off to the side, quickly draw a simple stick figure to represent Joseph. Then draw a coat outline around it. Let each child who wants to come up and color the coat a different color.

say ▸ Look at this gorgeous coat! Joseph's brothers were so jealous and angry that their father gave Joseph a beautiful coat and didn't give them beautiful coats. Joseph made his brothers even madder when he told them of his dreams. Close your eyes and pretend you're dreaming. Joseph said he dreamed that all the boys were working in the field. Suddenly, Joseph's plant of grain grew straight and tall. Have children stand and reach straight up with their arms as high as they can. Next, all of the brothers' plants gathered around Joseph's plant and bowed before him. Can you picture plants bowing to one another? Place one child in the center of the circle, and have the other children circle around with their arms straight above their heads. Instruct them to begin swaying and bowing toward "Joseph" in the center of the circle.

Well! When Joseph told this dream to his brothers, they knew what that meant. They weren't going to say that Joseph was better than they were, and they certainly were not going to bow down to Joseph. They laughed at the very thought of this happening. And it made them even more angry!

Then Joseph had another dream. This time Joseph dreamed the sun, moon, and 11 stars bowed before him. The sun and moon were Joseph's mom and dad. Who do you think the 11 stars were? Pause for kids to respond. The stars represented Joseph's brothers. Joseph's dad said to him, "Do you really believe that one day your mom, brothers, and I will bow down to you?" His brothers were very angry by now! But the Bible says Joseph's dad kept thinking about Joseph's dream. Quickly draw the sun and moon. As you draw the 11 stars, have children help you count.

Our big storytelling mural looks great! We drew some good pictures of what happened in our Bible story.

ask • Why do you think family members should show God's love to one another?

say God gave us our families to love and take care of us. We can show God's love to our family by helping, sharing, and not thinking we're better than anyone else. Families need to show God's love.

Crafts

Joseph's Coat

Supplies: blank "coat" template drawn on paper (make one, and copy it for the children), smocks, pencils, vinegar, bowls, colorful tissue paper, wet wipes, paintbrushes

Distribute the "coat" pages. Have kids write their names on their papers and put on smocks to protect their clothing. Pour about a ¼ cup of vinegar into each of the bowls. Set the bowls on the table, along with colorful tissue paper and wet wipes for kids to share. Each child also will need a paintbrush.

Let children tear small pieces of tissue paper and place the paper inside the outline of the coat. Have each child dip a paintbrush into the vinegar, tapping off the excess liquid. Then have the child dab the brush onto the tissue paper pieces, holding the tissue pieces in place as he or she works. Make sure all the tissue paper pieces are moist, and then set them aside to dry. Have children use wet wipes to remove the tissue color from their fingers if necessary. When the vinegar dries, carefully peel off the tissue pieces, and the color will remain on the paper.

ask • Why do you think Joseph's father gave him a colorful coat?

• How does your family show you love?

say One way Joseph's dad showed Joseph his love was by giving him a special coat. This made Joseph happy. We make others happy when we show them God's love. Families need to show God's love. And we need to love everyone in our family.

Loving Families

Supplies: construction paper, magazines, pencils, glue sticks

Set out magazines and glue sticks. Give each child a piece of construction paper, and help write his or her name on the paper. Have the children look through the magazines for pictures of families showing love and tear them out. Some examples are a child hugging a parent, a parent taking care of a sick child, a parent fixing a meal, children sharing toys, and families playing together or reading together. Have the children glue the pictures they find onto the construction paper.

ask
- **How do you feel when you do something fun with your family?**
- **How do you think God feels when you love other people?**
- **What's something your family can do this week to show how much you love one another?**

say You've just made a special picture showing how a family loves one another. When we show love to one another, it makes God happy. Families need to show God's love.

Games

Wake Up!

Supplies: none

Have children lie on a mat (or on the floor) and pretend to sleep like Joseph was sleeping when he had his dream. Tell the children that you're going to talk about ways that families can treat each other. If they hear a way that families are showing love to each other, they should "wake up!" (sit or stand up), but if they hear a way a family is not showing love, they should continue to "sleep." Alternate the two choices. Examples:

• Showing love: doing chores, helping with younger siblings, obeying parents, not arguing, using good manners.

• Not showing love: disobeying parents, arguing with siblings, not sharing, not putting things back where they belong, being unkind.

ask
- **What are some ways you can show love to the people in your family?**
- **What are some ways that God shows love to your family?**

say Joseph's family did not always do a very good job showing love to each other. Sometimes it isn't easy to show love to other people, but God will always help us if we ask him. Families need to show God's love.

PRayeRS

Lots of Love Prayer

Supplies: none

Say ▶ **We're going to go around the circle and name a family member who we can show God's love to this week.**

Go around the circle and let everyone share—don't forget to include yourself! Say the following prayer in these short, manageable phrases, and have the children repeat after you.

PRay ▶ **Dear God,**
Help me every day
To show your love
In a special way.
Help me to love
My family
And be the best
That I can be.
In Jesus' name, amen.

snacKS

Licorice Dream

Supplies: licorice ropes ("pull apart" kind)

Have kids wash their hands. Clean the table where children will eat their snack.

Explain that Joseph and his brothers did not always get along. When the brothers heard about Joseph's dreams, they felt jealous and angry. Distribute ropes of licorice to children, and have them begin pulling the strings apart. Divide extra ropes so each child has 12 pieces. Show kids how to position the 12 pieces to represent the plants in Joseph's dream, with one plant standing tall while other pieces bow down to it. While children are playing, lead the following discussion:

ask ▶ • **How could Joseph's family have shown more love for each other?**

• **How will you show love to your family this week?**

Say ▶ **Joseph's family did not always show love to each other. Sometimes our families forget to show God's love, too. That is why we are thankful God sent Jesus for us. He forgives us when we are unloving and helps family members forgive each other. Best of all, he promises to help us become more loving like him! Families need to show God's love.**

Team Mix

Supplies: small cups, plain M&M'S candies, pretzels, raisins

Set out small cups for the snack. The best way to complete this snack is to set up an assembly line, putting different children in charge of cups and each ingredient. Each child will put a small handful of one of the ingredients in the cup, and then pass the cup to the next child who will add the next ingredient, and so on. The child at the end of the line will pass out the filled cups.

Say ▷ **Families can show God's love by working together as a team. In your cups, you'll find M&M's. They remind us of Joseph's colorful coat. You also have pretzels that look like hugs we can give our families. Last, you have raisins that remind us of the dark night sky when Joseph was dreaming.**

SONGS

"Love One Another" Rhyme

Supplies: none

As you teach the children this active rhyme, remind them that even though Joseph's brothers treated him poorly, families need to show God's love to each other. Say the rhyme several times to allow the children the opportunity to learn the actions.

RHYME ▷ **Joseph's brothers didn't like the dreams he had.** *(Shake your head back and forth as if saying "no!")*

Those dreams made his brothers all feel very mad! *(Stomp your foot.)*

But don't be like them and always feel sad. *(Make a sad face.)*

We must love one another and be very glad! *(Hug a few friends.)*

JOSEPH IS SOLD INTO SLAVERY

Bible Basis:

Genesis 37:12-36

Supplies:

Bible, laundry basket or large box, child-size robe, fake gold coins, empty paper towel roll

Place a box or laundry basket in one corner of the room. You'll need one child-size robe and some gold coins.

Open your Bible to Genesis 37, and show children the words.

say **Today's Bible story tells us God wants us to do what is right. Raise your hand if your mom or dad watches the news on TV.** Pause for children to respond. **You can find out about big events that happen by watching the news. Let's pretend you're people in a news story and I am the news reporter.**

Choose children to be sheep, and have them crawl on the "grassy field." Tell them to walk around, quietly bleating, throughout the news. Choose boys and girls to be Joseph's brothers. Have the "brothers" walk among the sheep. Then choose one child to be Joseph. Have "Joseph" wear the robe and sit on the opposite side of the room from the basket or box. Have any other children pretend to be the Ishmaelites, and divide the coins among them. Have the "Ishmaelites" wait on the side of the room by Joseph. Give an empty paper towel roll "camera" to a child, and ask him or her to operate the camera. Turn toward the person with the camera, say "Action!" and begin.

say **Good evening, ladies and gentlemen. We have a breaking news report of an incident involving a young man named Joseph and his brothers. The story begins in a field, where the brothers are watching their father's flock of sheep.** Encourage the sheep to walk on the green field and bleat. Have the brothers walk around the sheep, occasionally reaching down to pet them.

Eyewitness reports say that Joseph's father sent Joseph to check on his brothers. Have Joseph walk slowly toward the brothers, meandering through the room to give the characters time to speak. Tell the brothers to say such things as "Here comes that dreamer" and "Look at that beautiful coat Joseph got from Dad." Have Joseph continue to walk around the room, not yet reaching the brothers, as you continue:

The brothers want to get rid of Joseph. They are so jealous of him. What will they do? Let's take a closer look. Have the brothers gather close together and whisper loudly, "Let's get rid of Joseph." Choose one child to be Reuben who says, "Let's not hurt him. Let's just throw him in a well for now."

Have Joseph walk over to the brothers.

say ▶ **Friends, look what's happening. Joseph is walking over to his brothers. His brothers are taking off his beautiful coat!** Motion for the brothers to remove the "coat." **The brothers put Joseph in a well!** Motion for the brothers to lead Joseph to the basket or box, and help him get inside. **God wants us to do what is right.**

ask ▶ • **Are they doing what's right?**

say ▶ **Our live newscast doesn't end yet! Here comes a gang of traveling Ishmaelites. What will the brothers do now?** Pause for children to respond. **Let's listen!** Direct the Ishmaelites to walk toward the box. Encourage the brothers to say, "Let's sell Joseph and get some money!" **God wants us to do what is right. Can you believe it? The brothers are selling Joseph so the travelers will take him away to be a slave.** Ask a brother to help Joseph out of the box. Direct the Ishmaelites to hand the brothers the coins and walk away holding onto Joseph's arms.

The brothers are leaving now to tell their father a lie. Have the brothers say, "Let's tell Dad that a wild animal must have eaten Joseph." Then have them guide their sheep to one side of the room. **Meanwhile, the Ishmaelites are going to Egypt to sell Joseph to an important person there. That's it for our live news report. I'm** [your name] **reporting live from the grassy field.** Set the props aside, and gather kids in a circle.

ask ▶ • **What wrong choices did the brothers make?**

• **Why were they wrong choices?**

• **What right choices can you make this week?**

say ▶ **Joseph's brothers were so jealous. They took his coat, threw him in a well, and then sold him to be a slave. We sometimes make wrong choices, too. God wants us to do what's right. Let's pray to God, and he'll help us make right choices.**

When Jesus was on earth he prayed to God to help him make right choices, too. Jesus asked God to show him the right thing to do and then asked him for the strength to do it. We can ask God for strength to do what is right just as Jesus did.

CRafts

Rainbow Chains

Supplies: strips of colored construction paper, crayons, stapler

say ▶ **Joseph's brothers were very jealous of him because their father loved him so much.** Ask the children to remember what special gift Joseph's father gave him, and encourage them to tell you.

Joseph's brothers decided to sell him to some men who were passing by. I am going to give each of you several different colors of construction paper. Draw a picture on each one of something that you can do that is right. Talk with the children about the fact that Joseph's brothers did not choose to do the right thing.

Joseph's brothers were mean and unkind to Joseph. They chose to sell Joseph and made some very bad choices. Even though Joseph's brothers were mean, God wants us to do what is right. After the children have drawn their pictures, show them how to link the strips of paper together to make a chain. Remind the children that Joseph was a slave and that often, slaves are put into chains to make sure they don't run away. Let the children try on their chains.

ask ▶ • **Is it easy or hard for you to do what is right? Why?**

• **Why do you think Joseph's brothers didn't do the right thing?**

say ▶ **This week when you think about doing the wrong thing, look at your chains and do one of the right things instead. And remember, God wants us to do what is right. If you are having a hard time choosing the right thing, pray and ask God to help you.**

Construction Site

Supplies: small paper plates, paper cups, glue sticks, brown and gray construction paper torn to look like stones

Give each child a small paper plate and a small paper cup. Set out glue sticks and the construction paper pieces for children to share. Explain to the children they will be making wells to take home so they can tell their families all about today's Bible story.

Demonstrate how to glue the paper pieces all around the outside of the cup as "stones." Then glue the bottom of the cup to the paper plate.

As children are working, discuss the following questions.

ask ▶ • **Why was it wrong for Joseph's brothers to put him in the well?**

• **How would you have felt if you were Joseph?**

say ▶ Joseph's brothers did a bad thing when they put him in the well. But we've learned that God wants us to do what's right. And that means being nice to our brothers and sisters. Take your wells home with you today so you can tell the Bible story to your families!

PRAYERS

What's Right Prayer

Supplies: none

Ask kids to each think of a right or good thing they want to do this week. Have each child say the good thing during prayer time. You will begin the prayer, and then pause for kids to add their ideas.

PRAY ▶ Dear God, help us to do what is right.

Please hear us as we tell you these right and good things we want to do this week. Pause while kids share.

We ask you to help us in all we say or do.

We love you.

In Jesus' name, amen.

Do What's Right

Supplies: none

Say the following prayer, pausing for the children to repeat after you.

PRAY ▶ Dear God,

I will try to do what's right

In the morning, noon, and night.

I will try to do what's right.

I will try with all my might.

In Jesus' name, amen.

snacks

Snacking Well

Supplies: napkins, plastic knives, prepackaged cream-filled cupcakes, teddy bear cookies

Encourage children to wash their hands before they prepare the snack, and then gather them around the supplies. Have each child cut the top off of a cupcake to form a well. Give each child a teddy bear cookie to place in the center of the well. Ask children to share what wrong choices the brothers made in the story and tell why God wants us to do what is right. Have a volunteer offer a prayer, and then let kids eat and enjoy their snacks.

Well, Well, Well

Supplies: marshmallow creme, bowls, paper plates, mini marshmallows, gummy bears

Have children wash their hands (or use wet wipes) and then gather together to make the snack. Spoon the marshmallow creme into several small bowls. Set the bowls out for children to share. Give each child a small paper plate and about 10 marshmallows. Explain that children will be making marshmallow "wells" to remind them of today's Bible story.

Demonstrate how to place some of the marshmallows in a circle on the plate. Then dip the bottoms of the other marshmallows in the marshmallow creme "cement" and place them on top of the first marshmallows to make the well.

Then give each child a gummy bear, and tell children to pretend the bear is Joseph. Children can place "Joseph" in the well and take him out again. Then let children enjoy their treats as you discuss the following questions.

ask · **Why did Joseph's brothers put him in the well?**

· **How do you think Joseph felt when his brothers put him in the well?**

· **How do you think God felt about what Joseph's brothers did?**

say **Joseph's brothers did a bad thing when they put Joseph in the well. But we know that God wants us to do what is right. We can choose to do what is right, not what is wrong. And God will help us do what's right. That's great news!**

JOSEPH FORGIVES HIS BROTHERS

Bible Basis:

 Genesis 42:1–45:28

Supplies:

Bible, resealable plastic bags, bowl of uncooked rice, measuring cup, empty bowl, cutout pictures of fancy meals from magazines

Open your Bible to Genesis 42, and show the children the words.

say ▶ **Today's Bible story teaches that you should forgive as God forgave you. God wants us to forgive.**

After Joseph's brothers sold him to some traveling men, they took him to Egypt to live. After several years, Pharaoh, who was the leader of the whole region, had a dream he couldn't understand. Joseph told Pharaoh that his dream meant there would be seven years of lots of food and then seven years with almost no food. When there's no food to eat, it's called a famine. Pharaoh was so happy to know what his dream meant that he put Joseph in charge of the planning. God helped Joseph save food.

When there was no food, many people came to Egypt to buy food from Pharaoh. One of those families that came was Joseph's family. Let's pretend that we're part of Joseph's family and that we have to travel far away to buy food for our family to eat.

(In a deep voice) **Our father, Jacob, said we must go buy food from Egypt. Come, my brothers.** Give each child a resealable plastic bag. Motion for the class to stand up and follow you.

Lead the children around the classroom, weaving in and out of tables and chairs, to show that it was a long journey to get to Egypt. When you get near the container of rice, stop and choose someone to be Joseph. Have "Joseph" stand on a sturdy chair at the rice container. Have the other children bow toward Joseph with you.

say ▶ (In a deep voice) **We have come to buy grain. May we please have grain?**

(In your own voice) **Now Joseph knew his brothers right away, but they didn't know it was him. Joseph asked his brothers about their family because he wanted to know about his younger brother and his father. The brothers said, "Our younger brother is home with our** father." And Joseph said, "You must leave one brother with me and bring your other brother here." Have each child use the measuring cup to put a scoop of rice from the container into his or her resealable plastic bag. Choose one child to stay with Joseph. Stand up and begin the journey back the same way you came, through the tables and chairs.

(In a deep voice) **Father, we're home with plenty of food.** Have the children pour their rice into an empty container and hold onto their empty bags. **But we must return to Egypt with our little brother, Benjamin.** Choose a smaller child to be Benjamin.

(In your own voice) **Jacob didn't want his sons to take Benjamin because he was afraid of what might happen. But soon, the family ran out of food again. So Jacob had to send his sons back to Egypt, this time with Benjamin.** Have children hold their bags, and again lead the group along the "path" to Egypt.

(In a deep voice) **We have returned to buy more food. We have brought our brother Benjamin, like you asked.** Have "Benjamin" stand in front of Joseph.

(In your own voice) **Joseph was so happy to see his younger brother Benjamin that he gave a big fancy dinner!** Show the children the magazine pictures of the fancy meals.

Have all the children sit down briefly and pretend to eat. Then have them use the measuring cup to put rice in their bags.

say ▶ **Joseph had lots of brothers to forgive, and he had many unkind things to forgive them for. But that didn't stop him from forgiving his brothers. Joseph forgave them and even had a big dinner in their honor. God never gets tired of forgiving us of our sins. God showed his forgiveness by sending Jesus to die for our sins. And because he forgives us, God wants us to forgive others.**

Later, Joseph told the brothers who he was. Joseph forgave his brothers for being mean to him and selling him to the travelers a long time ago. Joseph knew that God wanted him to forgive. He forgave his brothers and sent them back to get their father. Jacob was so happy to know his son was still alive that he went to Egypt to see him. Then all of Joseph's family moved to Egypt to live with Joseph. Joseph's family was together again! Have the children jump up and down, clap their hands, and hug one another to show their happiness.

ask ▶ • **How do you think Joseph's brothers felt when Joseph told them that he forgave them?**

• **How do you think God feels when we forgive others?**

- What is it like to know that God forgives you when you hurt others?

> **say** God forgives us when we do a bad thing. Because God forgives us, God wants us to forgive others.

BiBLe eXPeRiences

Celebration Meal

Supplies: modeling dough, paper plates

Set out modeling dough and paper plates. Let children make "food" out of the modeling dough to put on their plates, then re-enact the banquet meal with Joseph forgiving his brothers.

> **ask**
> - Why did the brothers need to go to Egypt?
> - Why did Joseph forgive his brothers?

> **say** The brothers went to Egypt to get some food. It might have been hard for Joseph to forgive, but he did. He knew God meant everything that happened for good. Just as God wanted Joseph to forgive his brothers, God wants us to forgive. The whole family celebrated by enjoying an awesome meal together.

CRafts

Feel Forgiveness

Supplies: paper, crayons, small hearts cut out of red paper, glue sticks

> **say** Our Bible story helps us know that God wants us to forgive. And God wants us to forgive even when it's hard. He wants us to forgive because he already forgave us. God wants us to forgive. Let's say that together: God wants us to forgive.

> **ask**
> - Have you ever told someone that you forgive him or her? What happened?
> - What do you think it means to forgive someone?

say ▸ When we forgive someone, we might say, "OK, I forgive you for hurting my feelings." The Bible says that God loved us so much that he forgives us because Jesus died on the cross for our sins. So we should forgive everyone who makes us feel bad. We've all made mistakes and sinned.

Distribute the paper, and have kids write their names on their papers. Ask children to draw a picture of someone who has hurt them and who they need to forgive. When they've finished drawing, have them say, "I forgive you," then glue a red heart to the page.

ask ▸ • Why do you think God wants us to forgive others?

say ▸ God wants us to forgive others because God has forgiven each one of us. We can honor God by forgiving others.

Games

Let's Forgive

Supplies: none

Have the children sit in a circle. Choose one person to be Joseph. "Joseph" will walk around the circle saying "brother" or "sister" as he or she lightly taps classmates on the head. When Joseph taps someone and says "forgive," that person will get up, run after Joseph, and try to tag him or her before Joseph reaches the empty spot. If the child isn't able to tag Joseph, that child becomes the next Joseph.

Prayers

God's Heart of Forgiveness Prayer

Supplies: dry-erase board, markers, erasers

Set out a dry-erase board, markers, and erasers. Have children each make a stick figure on the board to represent someone they need to forgive. Say the following prayer:

Pray ▸ Dear God,

Please help us forgive others who hurt us.

Please help us forgive and forget. Let children erase the stick figures they've drawn on the board.

We thank you so much that you love us and forgive us. Help us always love and forgive others. Draw a large heart on the board. Then have all the children say the last line of the prayer with you:

In Jesus' name, amen.

Echo Prayer

Supplies: none

Form two groups, and teach children this chanting echo prayer. Have one group say the words with you, and then have the second group echo the words back.

PRAY **Dear God,** (Dear God,)

Help me to forgive, (Help me to forgive,)

When others do me wrong. (When others do me wrong.)

Help me to forgive, (Help me to forgive,)

And sing a happy song. (And sing a happy song.)

In Jesus' name, amen. (Both groups together.)

snacks

A Walk of Forgiveness

Supplies: bowls, dry cereal, milk, spoons

Ask children to wash their hands before snack time. Set out bowls of dry cereal, containers of milk, and spoons. Help children find partners. Have one child in each pair pretend to be Joseph and the other child pretend to be one of Joseph's brothers. Have each "Joseph" sit at a table in front of a bowl of dry cereal. Have the "brother" walk up to Joseph and say, "I'm sorry that I hurt you, Joseph. Will you forgive me?" Then have Joseph respond, "I forgive you, my brother. God wants us to forgive." Then have each Joseph give each brother a bowl of cereal. Switch roles, and repeat. When each child in the pair has a bowl of cereal, remind kids that Joseph's family needed food so the brothers went to Egypt where Joseph lived. Ask a volunteer to pray, and then let the children eat and enjoy!

Happy-Face Snack

Supplies: rice cakes, plastic knives, paper plates, cream cheese, raisins

 Joseph forgave his brothers, and that made them very happy. Let's make happy faces on these rice cakes to remind us that when we forgive others, we're happy and so is God. God wants us to forgive.

Give each child a rice cake on a paper plate. Provide plastic knives, and allow children to spread softened cream cheese on their cakes. Then let them create happy faces with raisins.

"Forgiving Others" Rhyme

Supplies: none

As you teach the children this active rhyme, remind them that just as Joseph forgave his brothers, God wants us to forgive, too. Group the children in pairs to learn this active rhyme. Direct the children to start the rhyme with their backs to their partners.

RHyMe **Joseph forgave his brothers.** *(Pairs turn and face each other.)*

He took them by the hand. *(Shake hands.)*

We can forgive others. *(Pairs put their arms around each other's shoulders.)*

That is God's good plan. *(Pairs point up, with arms still around each other.)*

Moses Meets God at the Burning Bush

Bible Basis:

Exodus 2:11–3:20

Supplies:

Bible, photocopy of "Go Moses!" script on page 55

Before this session, enlist a man from your church to play Moses. Give him the script from page 55, and have him stand outside your meeting area until you're ready for him.

Open your Bible to Exodus 2, and show the children the words.

say **Today's Bible story teaches us that God can use us. We're going to be Moses' cheerleaders to remind him that he can do anything because God will give him strength.** During the story, encourage children to pump and wave their arms as they cheer.

When you see Moses start to shiver and shake, we'll stand up and say this cheer to him: "Go on, Moses, to Pharaoh. God can use you, GO, GO, GO!" Then sit back down again until you see Moses shake and shiver again.

Welcome "Moses," and introduce him to the children. Then allow him to tell his story as you lead children in the actions.

After Moses finishes talking to the kids, **say** **God wanted to use Moses to set his people free, but Moses was afraid. God chose to speak to Moses from a burning bush to get his attention and to show Moses that God can use anything.**

ask **• Why was Moses afraid to go to Pharaoh?**

• What did God do for Moses?

• Can you name a time you were afraid of someone?

say **God loves us so much that he gives us strength so he can use us. God can use you. When Jesus was here on earth, God gave Jesus strength to obey him even when he was afraid. If you're afraid to do something for God, ask him to give you the power. God can and God will!**

BiBLe eXPeRiences

Station CAN DO

Supplies: items for simple tasks, such as a simple puzzle, clothespin and container with mouth just large enough for it to fit, popcorn, tweezers, bowls, paper cups, or other ideas

Set out materials for the CAN DO exercises listed below. You can use the following suggestions or think of some on your own. Set up CAN DO stations around the table. Kids will rotate around the table to each station.

Some suggestions for CAN DO stations might be to complete a simple puzzle, drop a clothespin into the mouth of a container, transfer popcorn with tweezers from one bowl to the next, or build a tower out of paper cups (one stacked up, the next down). Make sure the tasks are simple enough for them to complete successfully.

ask • **How did you feel after each task?**

• **What jobs can you do at home for God?**

say **Your whole life will be filled with little and big jobs to learn. When God gives you the strength, you can do anything! God can use us!**

CRafts

Hot Branches

Supplies: paper, crayons, craft sticks, glue, cinnamon candies, candy corn

Distribute the paper, and have kids write their names on their papers. Tell children to design their pages to look like the burning bush might have looked. They can break the craft sticks in half and glue them to the pages as the branches. Then glue the flaming red, orange, and yellow candies to the pages as the flames. As the glue dries, have kids tell one another what they remember about the story.

ask • **How did God speak to Moses in the story?**

• **How does God speak to us today?**

say **God spoke to Moses through a burning bush. Amazing! God wanted Moses to go to Pharaoh and tell him to set the Israelites free from being slaves! God speaks to us today through the Bible, church, Christian friends, and prayer. God can use us to do many things, such as tell others about Jesus and show his love through our kind actions. It's exciting when God uses us to do his will!**

Burning Bushes

Supplies: sandpaper squares, cellophane (1 red and 1 yellow square per child), stapler

Give each child a square of sandpaper. Encourage children to feel the texture of the sandpaper.

Say > **This paper is called sandpaper. That's because it feels all bumpy and scratchy like sand. In today's Bible story, Moses went out to the desert where there was lots of sand.**

Give each child two squares of cellophane, one of each color. Hold your two cellophane sheets up for the children to see.

Say > **While he was in the desert, God talked to Moses from a burning bush. These colors of red and yellow can remind us of the colors of fire. And listen!** Gently crumple the sheets of cellophane together. **These colored sheets even sound like a crinkly fire.** Encourage children to crumple and crinkle their cellophane sheets. **Now let's make burning bushes on our deserts!**

Help children crumple each cellophane sheet and carefully and securely staple the cellophane to the sandpaper squares to form burning bushes. Then gather the children together in a circle with their crafts.

ask > **• How do you think Moses felt when he saw the burning bush in the desert?**

• How did God use Moses after that?

• How do you think God could use you this week?

Say > **God used Moses, and God can use us! Take your burning bush home with you to remind you of today's Bible story. Use your bush to tell your friends and family that God can use them, too!**

PRAYERS

Burning Bush Prayer

Supplies: red and yellow cellophane sheets (crumpled), flashlight

Set the crumpled cellophane over the lamp of the flashlight. Turn off your classroom lights, and turn on the flashlight so the "bush" glows. Have children repeat each line of the following prayer to God as they look at the pretend burning bush:

Dear God,

Please use us to do your will.

Help us show people how much you love them.

Help us tell others about Jesus.

In Jesus' name, amen.

- -

Huddle Prayer

Supplies: none

Have the kids join you in a prayer huddle. Explain that a huddle is how football players help one another get excited about a game.

 Dear God, thank you for bringing us together to learn how you used Moses. We know that you can use us, too. Thank you for giving us strength. Have all the kids put their hands in a pile and shout: **In Jesus' name, amen!**

snacks

Burning Bush Snack

Supplies: paper bowls, spoons, broccoli florets, vegetable dip, red food coloring

Have children wash their hands or use wet wipes.

Ask a child to thank God for providing the snack and wanting to use kids.

Show kids how to make a "burning bush" snack. Give children bowls, and let them put a small amount of vegetable dip into their bowls. Then place a drop of red food coloring in the dip, and stir the dip with a spoon. Let kids dip their treelike broccoli into the red dip so it looks as if it's in flames. Have children take turns telling parts of the story to one another while eating their snacks. Remind them that God can use us.

Moses Story Song

Supplies: none

Have the children sing "Moses Story Song" to the tune of "Here We Go 'Round the Mulberry Bush."

SING **God protected Moses, Moses, Moses.**
God protected Moses
And kept him safe you see!

God protects me every day, every day, every day.
God protects me every day
And keeps me safe you see!

God can use us anywhere, anywhere, anywhere.
God can use us anywhere,
So let him! Don't you see?

God can use us anywhere, anywhere, anywhere.
God can use us anywhere,
So let him! Don't you see?

"Cheerful Cheering" Rhyme

Supplies: none

As you teach the children this active rhyme, remind them that God used Moses even when he was afraid, and God can use us. Line chairs up in a row. Have the kids sit in the chairs, and teach them this cheer for Moses.

RHYME **Go, Moses, go** *(sit and slap thighs three times)*

Back to Pharaoh! *(Stand up.)*

Go, Moses, trust. *(Sit and slap thighs three times.)*

God uses us. *(Stand up.)*

Go, Moses, speak. *(Sit and slap thighs three times.)*

God uses the weak. *(Stand up.)*

Go, Moses, see *(sit and slap thighs three times)*

Your people set free! *(Jump up and raise hands.)*

Go Moses! Script

(Moses enters.)

Hello, children, my name is M-M-Moses. When I was a baby, I was laid in a basket and put in a river to stay safe from mean soldiers. God saved me in the river! When I was a young boy, I had to go live with the princess in the palace of the Pharaoh. She became my new mother. But I never forgot my real family and the real God who rescued me.

I ran away from Egypt, and now I'm just a shepherd caring for sheep. I got married and had two little boys. One day I was taking care of the sheep in the desert, and I saw a funny sight. There was a bush on fire, but it didn't burn up! I went closer to check it out. I heard a voice say, "Don't come any closer. I'm God."

I was afraid to look at God. He said, "I have seen my people treated as slaves. I am sending you to Pharaoh. You must tell him to let my people go free."

(Moses starts to shake.) "Who, m-m-m-me?" I asked. "Why would you want to use m-m-me? You mean I'm supposed to go all the way back to Egypt and ask Pharaoh to just set all God's people free? Then he won't have anyone to work for him anymore." *(Moses starts to shiver and shake.)*

OK, kids, I believe God can use me. I'll go to Pharaoh. God himself promised to be with me. Thanks for cheering me on and reminding me that I can do anything when God gives me the strength! Goodbye!

(Moses exits.)

Moses Pleads With Pharaoh

Bible Basis:

Exodus 7:14–12:31

Supplies:

Bible

Open your Bible to Exodus 7, and show children the words.

say ▶ **Today's Bible story tells us that nothing matches God's power.**

Moses went to Pharaoh and said, "God wants you to let his people go." Pharaoh said, "N-O, no!" Say that with me. Have kids repeat the phrase, "N-O, no!" **God had to show Pharaoh that he was more powerful. So God sent bad plagues to help Pharaoh change his mind. First God turned all Egypt's water into blood. It was red, you couldn't drink it, and it smelled awful! Do you think Pharaoh let the people go after that?** Pause. **Pharaoh said, "N-O, no!"** Have kids repeat the phrase, "N-O, no!" **But God kept his people, the Israelites, safe to show everyone that nothing matches God's power.**

Then God sent frogs all over the land. They covered everything! Let kids hop like frogs. **Do you think Pharaoh let the people go after that?** Pause. **Pharaoh said, "N-O, no!"** Have kids repeat the phrase, "N-O, no!" **But God kept his people, the Israelites, safe to show everyone that nothing matches God's power.**

Then God sent teeny, tiny gnats. Have kids pinch their pointer fingers and thumbs together and make small "bzzzzz" sounds. **Then he sent bigger flies!** Have kids make louder "bzzzzz" sounds and swat or clap their hands together. **Do you think Pharaoh let the people go after that?** Pause. **Pharaoh said, "N-O, no!"** Have kids repeat the phrase, "N-O, no!"

But God kept his people, the Israelites, safe to show everyone that nothing matches God's power.

God made the Egyptians' animals get sick. Let kids hold their stomachs and "moo" as if they have tummy aches. **Then he made the Egyptians have sores and owies.** Have everyone hold their knees as if they've skinned them. **God wanted Pharaoh to quit being mean to his people. He wanted Pharaoh to let his people go!** Ask kids to say, "Let my people go!" **Do you think Pharaoh let the people go after**

that? Pause. **Pharaoh said, "N-O, no!"** Have kids repeat the phrase, "N-O, no!" **But God kept his people, the Israelites, safe to show everyone that nothing matches God's power.**

So God sent big, icy balls of hail. Have kids cover their heads and say, "Ouch, ouch!" **Then he sent locusts that flew like flying grasshoppers! They ate up the fruit from the trees!** Have kids flap their arms like wings and make munching sounds. **Do you think Pharaoh let the people go after that?** Pause. **Pharaoh said, "N-O, no!"** Have kids repeat the phrase, "N-O, no!" **But God kept his people, the Israelites, safe to show everyone that nothing matches God's power.**

Pharaoh wanted to keep God's people and use them as slaves forever. So God sent darkness over the land. Let kids close their eyes. **It was soooo dark.** Let kids cover their closed eyes with their hands to make it even darker. **Do you think Pharaoh let the people go after that?** Pause. **Pharaoh said, "N-O, no!"** Have kids uncover and open their eyes, and then repeat the phrase, "N-O, no!" **But God kept his people, the Israelites, safe to show everyone that nothing matches God's power.**

Finally, God sent the last plague—the plague of death for the Egyptians. But God kept his people, the Israelites, safe to show everyone that nothing matches God's power. Do you think Pharaoh let the people go after that? Pause. **Finally Pharaoh said, "Yes! Get out of here and don't come back!" God had kept his people, the Israelites, safe and showed everyone that nothing matches God's power!**

ask • **How did God show his power in the story?**

• **How does God show his power to us today?**

say It's easy for us to forget that God can do anything. You and I can't create darkness. We can't tell the insects what to eat or make thousands of frogs hop around. What is impossible for you and me is easy for God because nothing matches God's power! Jesus demonstrated God's great power here on earth. He calmed the storm and performed amazing miracles in everyday life. Jesus wants you to experience God's power in your life, too.

Don't Be Afraid

Supplies: modeling dough

Set out a handful of modeling dough for each person. Tell each child to shape the dough into something he or she is afraid of, such as a big dog, a lightning bolt in a storm, or a bully. One at a time, have kids share their fears and then roll the dough into a ball as they say, "Nothing matches God's power."

ask • **How does God show his power when you're afraid?**

say **We don't need to be afraid because nothing matches God's power. He cares for each of us and knows what's best for us.**

Attractive Power

Supplies: magnets; metal objects such as paper clips, staples, metal washers, and screws

Place the metal objects on the table, along with several magnets. Form pairs, and have one child in each pair use a magnet to pick up a metal object. Then have the second child try to take the object off of the magnet using another magnet.

ask • **How did it feel when you picked up things with your magnet?**

• **How can God use his power to help you when you're afraid?**

say **God's power is like this magnet. He can pick up your fears and take them away. Nothing matches God's power.**

CRafts

Pack It Up

Supplies: paper, crayons or markers, magazines, newspapers, glue sticks, scissors

Distribute the paper, and have kids write their names on their papers. Set out magazines, newspapers, glue sticks, and scissors.

Ask children to cut out pictures of things they want to take on a long journey. Have them glue the pictures on their papers.

ask • **What do you think the Israelites took with them as they left Egypt?**

• **What would you take with you on a long trip?**

say **The Israelites must have packed just what they needed for a long trip—simple food, clothes, and their animals. God set the Israelites free from slavery! God's freedom lasts forever, because Jesus sets us free from our sin. Thank you, God!**

Back-to-School Bags

Supplies: brown lunch bags; ribbon; glue; various art supplies such as stickers, markers, and glitter

say **When the Israelites escaped from Egypt, they left their homes behind but took some belongings and even asked their Egyptian neighbors for valuable things to help them on their way. Today we're going to make bags to remind us that God is with us when we're away from home, just as he was with the Israelites.**

Provide art supplies, and distribute one bag per child. Be sure to help children put their names on their work. As children create, discuss the following questions.

ask • **Where will you take your bag?**

• **What will you carry in your bag?**

• **How do you feel knowing that God is always with you?**

• **How could you use your bag to tell others about God's love?**

When children are done decorating their bags, help them glue on the flat ribbon to make a handle on their bags.

say **Wherever you take your bag, remember God's people and his promise to set them free. We are glad that Jesus sets us free so we can follow and obey him.**

Games

We're Free!

Supplies: robe, suitcase, kitchen timer

Have children sit in a large circle with the suitcase open in the center. Let children choose one child to be Moses and to wear the robe. To begin, set the timer for 15 seconds (as kids get faster, set the timer for less time). Show "Moses" how to start the timer. Have Moses walk around the outside of the circle. When Moses is ready, have him or her stop and say, "Pack fast!" Then let him or her push the start button on the timer. Tell everyone to quickly take off their shoes and put them inside the suitcase. Tell kids not to close the suitcase because you don't want any fingers or hands hurt. Let the timer run out, and then choose a new Moses and begin the game again. Kids will want to each have a turn or two being Moses before you end the game.

ask • Why did the Israelites have to hurry?

• How do you think the Israelites felt about finally being freed from slavery to Pharaoh?

say When we sin, we should hurry to ask for forgiveness so we can feel free from our sins. The Israelites had to hurry to pack in case Pharaoh changed his mind. They wanted to escape from slavery as fast as possible. It feels good to be free! Jesus sets us free from our sin so we can live forever with him.

Prayers

Power Prayer

Supplies: none

Lead children in the following prayer. Then have kids add their prayers when you pause.

pray Dear God,

Help us remember that you're always with us. Have kids stand with arms around one another's waist or shoulders.

We ask for your power to protect us the next time we're afraid of… Have kids say their fears.

We give our fears to you.

In Jesus' name, amen.

Prayer at the Cross

Supplies: paper cross, tape

Tape a paper cross on the wall. Have the children come kneel before the cross and repeat this prayer after you.

PRay **Dear Jesus,**
Thank you for the love and care
You show to people everywhere.
Thank you, Lord, especially
That Jesus came to set me free!
In Jesus' name, amen.

snacks

Set Free Snack

Supplies: plates, crackers, M&M'S candies or raisins

Ask children to wash their hands before they prepare their snack.

Have children position crackers on their plates in a circle so it looks like a fenced-in area. Let kids place M&M'S or raisins in the center to represent the Israelites. Encourage children to retell the Bible story and then open the gate (remove a cracker) and set free each of the M&M'S. As children release each of the M&M'S, have kids say, "Jesus sets us free!"

Ask a child to say a prayer, and then let kids enjoy their snacks.

Passover Picnic Snack

Supplies: matzo crackers, white grape juice or purple punch

As you distribute pieces of matzo crackers and white grape juice or purple punch, have the children pretend they're God's people eating their last meal in Egypt. While they snack, let the children share one thing they would pack to take with them if they had to leave their homes.

say **The Israelites left Egypt in a hurry. They ate simple food and took**
whatever they could carry. They were probably excited and scared,
but they knew nothing matches God's power.

"Do Not Fear" Rhyme

Supplies: none

As you teach the children this active rhyme, remind them that we do not need to be afraid because nothing matches God's power. This is a clapping rhyme. Have the kids pat their hands on their legs twice and then clap their hands twice.

RHYME

Do not fear,
God is near.
He holds you tight
With all his might.
Every hour
God has power!
So do not fear
'Cause God is here.

MoSeS CRoSSeS tHe ReD Sea

Bible Basis:

Exodus 13:17–14:31

Supplies:

Bible, poly-fiberfill, masking tape, flashlight

Create the outline of the "Red Sea" on the floor using masking tape.

Open your Bible to Exodus 13, and show the children the words.

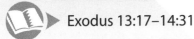 **say** ▶ **God set the Israelites free from slavery to Pharaoh and the Egyptians. Let's pretend that we're the Israelites going through the desert to our new home. It might be scary out here, but remember that God helps us when we're afraid.**

God made a bright cloud for the Israelites to follow during the daytime and a big cloud of fire—kind of like this flashlight—for them to follow at night. Let's pretend to follow God like the Israelites did. Have the kids stand up.

Take some poly-fiberfill, fluff it into the shape of a cloud, and hold it above your head so all the kids can see. Tell them it's daytime in the hot desert, and lead the children around the room.

Then pretend it's nighttime. Turn out the lights, tuck the flashlight inside the "cloud," and turn on the flashlight so that the cloud glows. Have the kids follow you around the room on a nighttime march to the Red Sea marked by masking tape.

say ▶ **The Israelites followed God during the daytime and nighttime. God helped them when they were afraid.** Turn the lights back on, and turn off the flashlight.

When the Israelites came to the Red Sea, they couldn't go across it because it was too deep. They couldn't jump over it because it was too wide. So the Israelites decided to go to sleep. They would try to solve this problem tomorrow. Have the kids pretend to sleep.

In Egypt, Pharaoh became angry and wanted his slaves back. So he ordered his army to go after the Israelites and bring them back.

Wake up, Israelites! Have the kids pretend to wake up. **The Israelites saw Pharaoh and his army coming to get them. They remembered their Red Sea problem, and they were so afraid! They didn't want to be Pharaoh's slaves again. What could they do?**

ask • What would you do if you were one of the Israelites?

say They cried out to Moses, and Moses cried out to God.

ask • Do you think God left his people? Why or why not?

say **God didn't leave his people. God helped them when they were afraid. He did an amazing thing. God told Moses to point his walking stick at the Red Sea.** Have kids hold up make-believe walking sticks. **All of a sudden God separated the deep waters so there was dry ground to walk on all the way to the other side!** Have the children follow you to the edge of the masking tape sea on the floor.

God helped the Israelites when they were afraid. Pharaoh and his army came after them, but all of the Israelites made it safely through the Red Sea to the other side. Lead the children through the Red Sea marked on the floor. Remind them to hurry because the Egyptians are coming!

The Egyptians started to go through on the dry ground, too, but the waters covered up Pharaoh and his army. When the children are safely on the other side, tell them to look back. **Look, everyone! The walls of water are closing. Pharaoh can't get us anymore. Let's praise God and give a big cheer!** Lead the children in clapping and shouting, "Yea, God!" **The Israelites were safe and free! God had saved them once again!**

Have the children sit in a circle, and ask them to imagine and share what they think it might have looked like when God parted the water and the Israelites crossed the Red Sea.

say **God helped them when they were afraid. God will help us when we're afraid, too.**

ask • How would you feel if someone chased you to hurt you?

• Do you think the Israelites felt the same way? Why or why not?

• What does God do for you when you're afraid?

say **God is so good! He saved the Israelites just like Jesus came to save us. When Jesus died on the cross, he made it possible for us to have a friendship with him. When we have Jesus for a friend, we don't have to be afraid of anything.**

BiBLe eXPeRiences

Dividing the Waters

Supplies: newspaper, small pitchers of water, cups

Cover a table with newspaper, then set out shallow pans, small pitchers of water, and cups. Let kids work in pairs (or individually), gently pouring water from the pitchers into the empty cups. Encourage kids to pour the water back and forth between the cups to make two cups with equal amounts of water. Remind the children that God divided the waters of the Red Sea so the Israelites could walk across on dry land.

ask • **How do you think the Israelites felt when God divided the waters in half?**

• **When has God been with you when you were afraid?**

say **God has promised to always be with us, and God helps us when we're afraid.**

CRafts

God Is With Me

Supplies: newsprint, paper, pencils, shallow bowls of water, watercolor paints, paintbrushes

Cover a table with newsprint, and have pencils, shallow bowls of water, watercolor paints, and paintbrushes on the table. Distribute the blank paper, and have kids write their names on their papers.

say **We're going to paint a picture of a time you were afraid and God was with you.**

ask • **What things make you afraid?**

• **What do you do when you feel afraid?**

• **When has God helped you to be brave?**

say **We all feel afraid sometimes. But God helps us when we're afraid.**

Run With God

Supplies: blue bedsheet

> **say** God helps us when we're afraid. Let's play a game to see how God helped the Israelites run on dry ground when they were afraid.

Direct half of your class to stand on both sides of a blue bedsheet and hold the edges, facing each other. Tell them they are the "Water People."

Direct the other half of the class to pretend to be the Israelites ready to cross the Red Sea. They will stand in a group at one end of the sheet. They are to call out, "God helps us when we're afraid!"

The Water People will hold the blue sheet above their heads and call out, "Run, run, you've got it made. God helps us when we're afraid!"

The "Israelites" will run under the blue sheet from one end to the other. The Water People will drop the sheet back to the ground. Have everyone cheer and call out again: "God helps us when we're afraid!"

If you have time, direct children to trade places so the Water People are now the Israelites and the Israelites are the Water People. Repeat the game again.

> **ask** • What were the Israelites afraid of?
>
> • How did God protect them?
>
> • How does God protect you?

> **say** We don't need to cross the Red Sea, but we have other things we need that God can give us. We can pray to God and tell him when we're afraid, and he will give us what we need.

PRAYERS

Action Prayer

Supplies: blue bedsheet

Ask someone to help you hold up a blue bedsheet to represent the Red Sea. Allow each child the opportunity to walk under the sheet with a partner and pray, "Dear God, thank you for being with me when I'm afraid. In Jesus' name, amen."

snacks

A Fruit Split

Supplies: newspaper or a plastic tablecloth, cups, spoon, large bowl, tub of whipped topping, fruit (bananas, pears, peaches, or canned fruit halves work well), paper plates, plastic forks and knives

Cover a table with newspaper or a plastic tablecloth. Tell children to wash their hands, then have them sit at the table to prepare their snacks. Set out cups, a spoon, a large bowl, a tub of nondairy whipped topping, and fruit.

Give kids paper plates and plastic knives and forks. Let children choose the fruit they would like to split (cut in half) for your classroom fruit splits. Show the kids how to hold their knives and forks to cut up the fruit pieces. Encourage kids to continue cutting the fruit in half until they have bite-size pieces. After they have finished cutting the fruit, have kids put the pieces in a large bowl, and let them take turns gently mixing the fruit. Have children scoop some of the fruit into their cups and add a spoonful of whipped topping.

As they enjoy eating their fruit snacks, remind children that God split the waters of the Red Sea so the Israelites could walk across safely.

ask • How difficult was it to cut the fruit for your snack?

• Do you think God had a hard time dividing the water in half for the people to get across? Why or why not?

• When has God kept you safe when you were afraid?

say God may not have to split the waters of a sea for us to get across, but God helps us when we're afraid any time we ask him to.

Yogurt-Split Snack

Supplies: spoons, clear plastic cups, vanilla yogurt, blue powdered-drink mix

Have the children wash their hands or clean them with wet wipes and then sit down to prepare their snack. Give children spoons and clear plastic cups. Fill half of each cup with vanilla yogurt, and then add about a teaspoon of blue powdered-drink mix. Let the children create "oceans" by mixing the two ingredients together. Encourage kids to separate their yogurt "seas" as they eat to imitate God parting the waters of the Red Sea.

ask
- **When have you felt brave?**
- **How did God help the Israelites to be brave?**

say **Even when the Israelites were afraid, God helped them walk bravely to the other side of the Red Sea. Let's thank God for giving the Israelites what they needed and for giving us our snack.** Invite a child to pray for the snack.

JERICHO'S WALLS COME DOWN

Bible Basis:

Joshua 6:1-27

Music-and-March Power

Supplies: Bible, blocks or boxes, noisemakers

Before you begin the Bible story, have the children help you use blocks or boxes to build a circular wall to be the wall of Jericho.

Have children sit outside the "wall of Jericho." Open your Bible to Joshua 6, and show children the words.

say ▸ **Today's Bible story tells us that God is powerful.**

The Israelites had been traveling through the desert for a long, long time. Then God told them they were ready to move into the land he'd promised them. But look! What's this? Point to the boxes representing the wall of Jericho. **There's a great big, huge wall all around the city called Jericho.**

How could the Israelites possibly get into the city with a great big wall around it? They couldn't go over the wall. They couldn't go under the wall. And they sure couldn't go through the wall.

God told the Israelites to march around the wall once a day for six days. Let's sing a song while we march around the wall.

Have children stand in a circle around the wall. Lead them in singing "The Israelites Go Marching" to the tune of "The Ants Go Marching."

sing ▸ **The Israelites marched 'round and 'round.** *(March around the wall.)*

Hurrah! Hurrah! *(Raise your arms over your head and shake your hands.)*

The Israelites marched 'round and 'round. *(March around the wall.)*

Hurrah! Hurrah! *(Raise your arms over your head and shake your hands.)*

The Israelites marched 'round and 'round *(march around the wall)*

Because God said he'd knock the wall down *(stomp with the rhythm)*

If they just kept marching 'round and 'round and 'round and 'round. *(March around the wall.)*

Have children gather around you again.

say On the seventh day, God told the Israelites to march around Jericho seven times. The first six times they marched around, they blew trumpets. On the seventh time around, they blew trumpets and shouted. Let's march around the wall seven times just like the Israelites did.

Distribute noisemakers.

Lead the children in walking around the wall. Count each circle you make, and remind kids to make noise with the noisemakers each time. The seventh time around, have kids use the noisemakers and shout. Then gently knock down the boxes to represent the wall of Jericho falling.

say The walls of Jericho came tumbling to the ground, so the Israelites were able to go into the city. God is powerful!

ask • What did God use to knock down the great big wall?

• How do you think the Israelites felt when God knocked the wall down?

say God cared about the Israelites, so he used his power to help them. God is powerful, and he uses his power to help you, too. Jesus used his power here on earth to heal the sick. When we are sick, we can ask Jesus to use his power to make us feel better. Jesus is powerful and cares for us.

CRafts

Trumpets of God

Supplies: sugar ice-cream cones, construction paper, masking tape

 say In our Bible story, we learned that God gave the city of Jericho to the Israelites in an awesome way. God told Joshua and his men to walk around the city once a day for six days. Then on the seventh day, God told the priests to blow their trumpets and the people to shout. The Israelites had to remember that God is powerful and believe that God would do as he said. On the seventh day, the people obeyed God, and the walls of Jericho came tumbling down. Let's make pretend trumpets to remind us that God is powerful.

Give each child a sugar ice-cream cone and one sheet of construction paper. Have children roll their construction paper, short side to short side. Once their papers are rolled into tubes, help the children fit the "handle" part of each cone into one end of the paper, adjusting the paper to fit tightly. Use masking tape to secure the edge of the construction paper. Also use masking tape to attach the cone to the edge of the paper.

Re-enact the Bible story, using the trumpets children made.

ask • How did God show that he is powerful?

• What mighty things can God do for you?

say Let's remember that God is powerful.

Leaning Tower of Pasta

Supplies: bowl of wagon-wheel pasta, 3x3-inch cardboard squares with a hole cut in the center and a length of string or yarn tied under the cardboard and pulled through the hole

Set out a bowl of wagon-wheel pasta on a table. Give each child one of the cardboard squares you prepared before the lesson, and show the children how to thread the end of the string through the center of a piece of pasta. Give each child a chance to thread several pieces of pasta onto his or her string. Make sure kids leave several inches of string free on top of their stacks of pasta. Tie a large knot on the end of the string so the pasta can't come off.

Show the children how to make the walls of Jericho by holding the cardboard base on the floor and pulling the string straight up. Then have them knock the tower over with their fingers. Show them how to rebuild the walls by holding the string straight up again.

ask • How did God show his people that he was powerful?

• What other powerful things can God do?

• How can God help you with his power?

say God is powerful, and God showed that power by knocking down the walls of Jericho. God can show power in your life, too, by helping you when you need him.

Games

Jericho's Walls, Walls, Fall

Supplies: drum

Clear the game area of any obstacles. Have everyone stand in a circle. Choose one child to be "Joshua." Instruct him or her to walk around the outside of the circle, touching each child's shoulder while saying "wall." Let the children know that when *you* make a loud noise with the drum and say the word "fall," everyone except Joshua and the person tagged must sit down quickly. Joshua and the other child then race around Jericho, trying to get to the opening in the wall first. If Joshua is tagged, the other child becomes Joshua. If Joshua is not tagged before getting back to the spot where he or she started, he or she remains Joshua when everyone stands to play again. If someone has been playing Joshua for more than two turns, allow him or her to pick a Joshua replacement to give others a turn, too.

ask • Why couldn't Joshua get into the city?

• Who knocked down the walls of Jericho?

say Joshua needed God's help to get into Jericho. No wall can stand up against God, and no wall can keep God out. Because God is powerful, Joshua was able to walk into Jericho without doing anything to the walls himself.

God Powered

Supplies: turkey baster, paper fan, straws, table tennis balls

Let the children use the straws, paper fan, and turkey baster to experiment with moving the table tennis balls with air.

ask ▶ • **Can you see the power that's moving the balls?**

• **How do we know that the power of air is at work?**

• **Even though we can't always see God's power, how do we know that God's power is at work?**

say ▶ **We don't see the air itself, but we see how the air moves the balls. In the same way, we don't see God, but we can see what his power does in our world. God is powerful, and he helps people feel brave, love each other, and do the right things. God also made our whole world—including you and me.**

PRAYERS

Powerful Prayer

Supplies: none

Have children form a circle. Allow children the opportunity to flex their muscles and pray one at a time, "Dear God, thank you for being so powerful. In Jesus' name, amen."

Jericho's Walls

Supplies: small plates, whipped cream cheese, graham crackers

Have kids wash their hands before beginning. Spread about ½ inch of whipped cream cheese on small plates. Pass out the plates, along with graham crackers, to the children. Have kids stand the crackers up in the cream cheese on the long sides to build the walls of Jericho. First have kids try to knock over the treats by shouting at them. Then have kids try to blow them down. Remind them that God is the one who is powerful enough to make anything fall down.

 • **Why do you think there were walls around the city of Jericho?**

• **Could the Israelites knock down the walls around Jericho by themselves? Why or why not?**

say **God is powerful, and God cared for the Israelites just like he cares for you.**

Ruth Trusts God

Bible Basis:

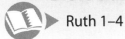

Ruth 1–4

Supplies:

Bible, large bowl, small bowl, pretzel sticks, wheat cereal squares, napkins

Before you begin, have the children wash their hands and sit at a table or in a large circle on the floor, close enough to reach the center. Hand out napkins for kids to place in front of themselves. Place a large bowl of pretzel sticks in the center of your children, along with a smaller bowl of wheat cereal squares. Tell the children they'll be helping you act out the Bible story with pretzel sticks. They will hold up one pretzel stick at a time when you add people to the story and then lay the pretzel sticks down as people leave the story. At the end, let the children eat all the pretzels.

Open your Bible to Ruth 1, and show children the words.

say ▶ **A long time ago in Bethlehem, there was a woman named Naomi.** Have each child take one pretzel stick from the bowl and hold it up. **Naomi married a nice man, and she was very happy.** Have each child take another pretzel stick and hold it up. **Naomi and her husband had one bouncing baby boy. Happy Naomi got even happier.** Have each child take another pretzel stick and hold it up. **Then they had another bubbly, bouncing baby boy.** Have each child take another pretzel stick and hold it up. **Naomi never dreamed she could be so happy. One, two, three, four in the happy family.** Have kids count their pretzel people.

The boys grew up, and they got married to two sweet ladies. Have each child take two more pretzel sticks and hold them up. **Now Naomi had a family of one, two, three, four, five, six.** Have kids count their sticks.

One day something very sad happened. The father died. Have each child put one pretzel stick down. **Later on, the two boys died.** Have each child put two pretzel sticks down. **Now there were only one, two, three in Naomi's family.** Have kids count the sticks in their hands. **Naomi never dreamed she could be so sad.**

She lived far away from all her friends and the rest of her family, and she felt lonely. Naomi said, "I'm going home. You girls can stay here with your own families." Naomi kissed them goodbye, and they

all cried. Have each child pick up one pretzel from his or her hand and touch it to the others as if giving them a goodbye kiss, and then place it back in his or her hand.

One daughter said, "OK, goodbye." Have each child put down one pretzel stick with the others.

Naomi started to walk away, all alone. She had never been lonelier. But the other daughter named Ruth ran to her and said, "I will stay with you. Wherever you go, I will go, and your God will be my God."

> **ask** • How do you think Naomi felt when she heard that?

> **say** **Ruth helped Naomi feel happier. There were only two left in Naomi's little family, but she felt better already!** Have kids count the sticks left in their hands.

Ruth and Naomi walked and walked for days. By the time they got to Naomi's town, they were hungry and had no more food left. So Ruth went out to a field to pick up grain that no one wanted. She knew that if she picked up enough grain, she could grind it into flour and make bread for her and Naomi to eat. Have each child pick up a few pieces of wheat cereal. **Ruth brought the food home to Naomi. They made bread and had a good dinner.**

Boaz, the man who owned the field, saw Ruth and wanted to help her. Naomi knew Boaz also needed a wife, so she sent Ruth to him. Ruth and Boaz liked each other and got married. Have each child pick up one pretzel stick to put with the others in his or her hand. **Now Naomi, Ruth, and Boaz were a very happy family.** Have the children count the sticks in their hands.

Later they had a bubbly, bouncing baby boy. Have each child add one more pretzel stick to his or her hand. **Now there were one, two, three, four people in Naomi's family.** Have the children count the sticks in their hands.

When this little boy grew up, he had more and more children. God blessed Naomi and Ruth because they chose to trust him. Allow kids to eat their pretzel sticks and cereal.

> **ask** • When did Naomi and Ruth have to trust God?
>
> • When do you trust God?

> **say** **Naomi and Ruth trusted God to take care of them when they were far away from their families and when they were sad. God gave them a new family, and everyone was happy again. We can trust God, just as Ruth and Naomi did.**

CRafts

Supplies: paper, straws, scissors, small bowls, glue

Cut the straws into one-inch lengths. Set out paper for each child and write the children's names on them. Set out straws and small bowls of glue.

asK ▸ • **What was Ruth looking for in the field?**

Remind children that Ruth picked up grain in Boaz's field. Explain that the grain was on long sticks, kind of like straw or dry grass. Show children how to dip the straw pieces in the glue and place them on their papers to represent all the grain that Ruth collected.

asK ▸ • **How did God help Ruth?**

▸ • **Do you believe that God will take care of you? Why?**

say ▸ **When we have hope in God, we know that God will take care of us.**

Let Hope Grow!

Supplies: clear plastic cups, index cards, magazines, glue, potting soil, seedlings

Give each child two clear plastic cups and an index card. Have children look through the magazines and each tear out a picture of good things God has given them, such as families, a new house, a pet, or sunshine. Then have children glue the pictures on their index cards.

When children have finished gluing their pictures, let each child describe his or her picture to the rest of the class. Then help each child tape the picture to the outside of one plastic cup. Next, place a bit of craft glue on the bottom of the cup with the picture, and carefully place it inside the second cup to make a picture planter.

Fill each cup with potting soil, and help each child plant a seedling in the cup. Gently water each plant.

asK ▸ • **What do you hope will happen to your little plant?**

▸ • **What do you need to do to help that hope come true?**

say ▸ **To help your little plant grow, you'll need to give it water and sunshine. God knows exactly what we need to grow! We can put all our hope in God, just like Ruth did. Take your little plant home to remind you that you can put your hope in God.**

PRAYERS

Hope Prayer

Supplies: drinking straws

Scatter drinking straws on the floor, enough so there is at least one straw for each child.

say ▶ **Ruth hoped in God, and God helped her find Boaz's field, where there was plenty of good grain for her.** Let's take turns picking up a straw and asking God to help us hope in him.

Let children take turns picking up straws and saying, "Dear God, help me hope in you." Collect the straws from the children.

PRay ▶ **Lord, we're glad that we can put our hope in you. Thank you for being a good God who we can trust. In Jesus' name, amen.**

snacks

A Snack of Grain

Supplies: whole grain cereal (such as Wheaties), snack-sized plastic bags

Before class, place a handful of cereal into each plastic bag, and hide the bags around the room. Make sure you have enough for each child to have one.

Have children pretend to be like Ruth and look around the room for the "grain." When everyone has found a bag, have children wash their hands (or use wet wipes) then sit down to eat their snack.

ask ▶ • **What did you hope to find as you looked around the room?**

• **How do you think Ruth felt when she found lots of grain in Boaz's field?**

• **How do you feel when God gives you the things you need?**

say ▶ **Let's thank God that we can put our hope in him and for providing our snack.** Invite one child to pray for the snack.

Ruth Hopes in God

Supplies: none

Lead children in singing "Ruth Hopes in God" to the tune of "The Farmer in the Dell."

SING ▶ **Ruth picks the grain.** *(Pretend to gather "grain" from the ground.)*
Ruth picks the grain. *(Pretend to gather "grain" from the ground.)*
Ruth hopes in God *(point up),*
So she picks up the grain. *(Pretend to gather "grain" from the ground.)*

Boaz cares for Ruth. *(Pat a friend on the back.)*
Boaz cares for Ruth. *(Pat a friend on the back.)*
Ruth hopes in God *(point up),*
So Boaz cares for Ruth. *(Pat a friend on the back.)*

Boaz marries Ruth. *(Hug a friend.)*
Boaz marries Ruth. *(Hug a friend.)*
Ruth hopes in God *(point up),*
So Boaz marries Ruth. *(Hug a friend.)*

ask ▶ • **What happened when Ruth hoped in God?**

• **Why can we hope in God?**

say ▶ **God gave Ruth everything she needed because she hoped in God. When we hope in God, he will give us all we need, too. You can always put your hope in God.**

Samuel Listens to God

Bible Basis:

1 Samuel 3:1-21

Supplies:

Bible, streamers cut into 5-foot lengths, tape, blanket, cutout footprints (1 set per child)

Before you begin your story, cut streamers to 5-foot lengths, one for each child. These will be "ephods." Spread out a blanket in one corner of the room to be Eli's "bed."

Open your Bible to 1 Samuel 3, and show the children the words.

say ▸ **Today's Bible story tells us to listen to God like Samuel did.**

When Samuel was a boy, his mother took him to live somewhere very special. Can you guess where Samuel lived? Give the children a chance to guess. **Samuel didn't live in a house or an apartment or a tree or a trailer. He lived in God's house! It was like our church, and they called it the Temple. You're going to pretend to be Samuel, the boy who served God.**

Samuel wore a special vest. Only people who served in the Temple were allowed to wear it. Put an "ephod" on each child. Crisscross a streamer over each child's chest and tape it in back. **This shows that you are a servant of the Lord.**

In those days, God didn't speak to people very often. But one night, something amazing happened! Eli the priest was sleeping in his usual place. I'll pretend to be Eli, sleeping over here. Lie down on the blanket. **You will all pretend to be Samuel, sleeping over there.** Have all the children lie down, pretending to be Samuel. It's a good idea to have children lie down side by side. This way no one gets kicked in the head while pretending to sleep!

Samuel was lying down when the Lord called him, "Samuel, Samuel!" Samuel jumped up and ran over to Eli. He shook Eli, saying, "Here I am. You called me." Have the children act this out.

Eli said, "I did not call; go back and lie down." So Samuel went back and lay down. Send the children back to their places, where they'll lie down.

Again the Lord called, "Samuel! Samuel!" Samuel got up, went to Eli and said, "Here I am. You called me." Let the children come and "wake" you.

"My son," Eli said, "I did not call; go back and lie down." Send the children back to lie down. **The Lord called Samuel a third time.** Let the children "wake" you again. **This time Eli realized that it was the Lord calling the boy. So Eli told Samuel, "Go and lie down, and if God calls you, listen to him. Say, 'Speak, God, for your servant is listening.'" So Samuel went and lay down in his place.** Send the children back to lie down. **He listened for God's voice.**

The Lord came and stood there, calling, "Samuel! Samuel!" Then Samuel said, "Speak, God, for your servant is listening." Have the children repeat this phrase together.

And the Lord spoke to Samuel. God told him that he was upset because Eli didn't stop his own sons from being bad. Samuel listened to God. In the morning Samuel told Eli everything that God had said. Gather children in a circle. **The Lord was with Samuel as he grew up, and people believed that what Samuel said was truly from God. Samuel helped people put their hope in God.**

ask • **Which way did Samuel go when he first heard God's voice?**

• **Then which way did he go?**

• **What about the second time?**

As you ask these questions and the children point first at Eli, and then back to the bed, and then back to Eli again, have them lay the footprints on the floor in front of them in the direction that Samuel walked each time. Then they can switch the directions of the footprints to indicate which way Samuel walked.

ask • **What did Samuel finally do?**

Encourage the children to kneel.

say **Speak, Lord, for your servants are listening.**

ask • **Who spoke to Samuel at night?**

• **What did Samuel need to do?**

• **If God talked to you, what would you do?**

say **God knows that children are important. Sometimes children listen to God better than big people! Samuel did the right thing when he answered, "Speak, God, for your servant is listening" and then listened to God.**

Crafts

What's That Sound?

Supplies: plastic spoons, string or yarn, one metal spoon

Help each child tie string around a plastic spoon handle so the spoon is hanging bowl-side down from the middle of the length of string. (As the child holds the two ends of the string, it should look something like a stethoscope.)

say In today's Bible story, Samuel heard a sound, but he didn't know what it was. Let's do a little experiment about sound.

Tap a metal spoon against the edge of a table, and let children listen to the sound it makes.

ask • Do you think you'll get the same sound if you tap your own spoon against the table? Why do you think that?

say Sometimes things aren't always what they seem—or sound! Let's try it!

Let each child take a turn placing the ends of the string on the outside of his or her ears (like a stethoscope) and gently swinging the string so the spoon hits the table. Children will be amazed when they hear a sound like a church bell, rather than the sound they heard when you tapped the table.

say When you listened through the string, you didn't expect to hear a sound like a bell, did you? Today in our Bible story, Samuel heard a voice he didn't expect—God's voice!

Samuel learned to listen to God. We can listen to God, too! Take your string with you, and when you get home, tie in a metal spoon so you can show your family this little experiment. Tell them the story of Samuel, and remind them that we can all listen to God!

Games

Listen to the Leader

Supplies: none

Play a game of "Listen to the Leader." Choose one child to whisper to another child an action such as "touch your nose and stand on one foot." The child who received the directions will start doing the action, and then the rest of the class should follow. Make sure each child gets a chance to whisper directions as well as to receive directions. Remind the kids that in today's Bible story they heard about a little boy who listened when God spoke to him.

PRAYERS

Listening Prayer

Supplies and Preparation: Create cards with drawing or pictures of children doing things (such as chores, acts of kindness, and so on).

Let each child choose a card. If you have more children than cards, have children each take one card then return the card to the pile. Have each child say a prayer similar to the following one, corresponding to what is on his or her card. Use your own name in your sample prayer. For example, if your card shows someone scrubbing a floor,

PRAY ▸ **Speak, God, for your servant,** [your name]**, is listening. I will listen to you, even if you tell me to** [scrub a floor]**. In Jesus' name, amen.**

SNACKS

Pepper Ears Snack

Supplies: paper plates, thin slices of green or sweet yellow peppers, carrots cut into thin julienne strips, raisins or tiny circle crackers

Have the children wash their hands (or use wet wipes) then sit down to prepare their snack. Give each child a paper plate to use as a "face." Set out the food, and show children how to lay down the green pepper ears, carrot noses, and circle eyes.

ask ▸ • **Why did God give us ears?**

• **What can we do with our ears?**

• **How do our ears help us to obey God?**

say ▸ **Let's thank God for our ears to listen to God and for providing our snack.** Invite one child to pray for the snack.

DaViD BeComes KinG

Bible Basis:
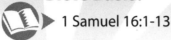

1 Samuel 16:1-13

Supplies:

Bible, paper crown

Open your Bible to 1 Samuel 16, and show the children the words. Before starting the story, tell the smallest child to be David. He or she will stay on the other side of the room until it's time to meet Samuel. The other children will pretend to be Jesse's other sons and will parade during the story.

say ▶ **Today's Bible story tells us that God doesn't care how we look.**

Samuel was a special man of God. He always tried to do just what God wanted him to do. He was a special messenger for God to the people. God talked to Samuel.

God was unhappy with King Saul. God asked Samuel to help find a new king. God told Samuel to go meet a man named Jesse, who had many sons. Jesse had his sons walk before Samuel, showing off how great they were. Each one looked like a king.

Some were tall. Have the children stand, then show them how to walk on their tiptoes. **Some were very strong!** Let children flex their muscles several times. **They were all very good-looking.** Have the children parade in a circle, smiling big, while you ooh and aah.

Samuel looked at each of them and thought, "This one looks like a king!" Bring out the crown and start to place it on the heads of several children. Stop each time and shake your head. **Each time, God said, "No—this is not the one."** God doesn't care how people look. When Samuel had seen them all, he asked Jesse, "Are all of your sons here?" Jesse said, "No—my youngest son is watching the sheep."**

Have all the children sit down except the smallest child, who may now come and stand before the group.

say ▶ **When Samuel saw David, Jesse's youngest son, he thought that David seemed smaller than the others. But God told Samuel, "This is the one who will be king." Samuel learned that what we look like isn't important to God; God doesn't care how we look. Let's all say that together. God doesn't care how we look.** Place the crown on "David's" head.

ask • How did Jesse's older sons look?

• How do you feel when people look at you and say you're too small to do something?

• Why did God choose David?

say God doesn't care how we look; he only cares about what's on the inside. God didn't have any trouble picking out the right brother for the job. He led Samuel right to him! God knows us better than anyone because God knows who we are in our hearts. Other people think they know us because they can see what we look like, but God doesn't care how we look. The Lord looks at the heart.

Bible Experiences

Supplies: dress-up clothes, basket

Before class, gather some dress-up clothes, and place them in a basket. Encourage kids to choose one of the outfits and try it on. Let the kids mill around for a while, changing clothes. When they have finished, remind them that they learned that it doesn't matter what you look like on the outside; God only cares about who you are on the inside.

- -

God Looks at the Heart

Supplies: hard-boiled egg, white construction paper torn into small pieces to look like bits of eggshell (a half to a full sheet of torn paper per child), colored construction paper, glue

Gather children around a table. Hold up a hard-boiled egg for them to see.

ask • What is this?

• What makes a hard-boiled egg taste good? This outside part? Tap the shell.

say Oh, it's not the shell that makes the egg taste good? It's the inside of the egg that makes the egg taste good. Crack the eggshell and peel it away from the hard-boiled egg. **That reminds me of our Bible story today. God didn't look at the outside of David to choose him as king. God looked at the inside. Let's make something to remind us that God doesn't care how we look—he cares about what's in our hearts.**

Give each child a sheet of colored construction paper and a supply of white paper bits. Explain that the paper bits look like broken eggshells. Let children glue the paper bits in a heart shape on the construction paper.

say When you look at your heart made of eggshell papers, remember the hard-boiled egg. It's the inside of the egg that tastes good, not the outside. God doesn't care what we look like on the outside. God knows the best things are inside us!

CRafts

Supplies: papers with a heart outline (make one "original" and then copy for your children), crayons or markers, 5x7-inch pieces of paper, tape

Distribute the full sheets of paper, and write the children's names on them.

Let children color the hearts on their papers. Then set out 5x7-inch sheets of colored paper and let children draw pictures of themselves. Tape the self-portraits on top of the hearts, so children can lift the picture and see the heart.

ask
- **Why did God choose David to be the king?**
- **Did God care that David was smaller than his brothers?**
- **Is it important to God how you look?**

say God made our bodies, so he loves how we look. But it's most important that our hearts are filled with God's love and kindness. God doesn't care what we look like. God looks at the heart.

PRayeRs

Heart-Filled Thanks

Supplies: small hand mirror

Form a circle, and pass around a small hand mirror. Let each child look in the mirror and say the following prayer, "Dear God, thank you for making me. I'm glad you look at my heart."

pRay Help us to fill our hearts with your love and kindness. In Jesus' name, amen.

The Inside Is What Counts

Supplies: graham crackers; plastic knives; paper plates; jelly; toppings such as mini marshmallows, raisins, chocolate chips, and colorful sprinkles

Have the children wash their hands (or use wet wipes) then sit down to prepare their snack. Give each child two graham cracker squares. Set out the jelly and several toppings such as mini marshmallows, raisins, chocolate chips, and colorful sprinkles. Let children spread jelly and a variety of toppings on one graham cracker then cover it with the other cracker. Walk around and try to guess what's inside each snack.

ask
- **Why did you choose to put those things inside your snack?**
- **How can someone find out what's inside your snack?**
- **How will people know what good and kind things are in your heart?**

say **God doesn't care what we look like. He wants our hearts to be like this snack—filled with wonderful, good things!**

Invite a child to pray for the snack.

DAVID DEFEATS GOLIATH

Bible Basis:

  1 Samuel 17:1-50

David Does a Great Thing

Supplies: Bible, stepstool, male guest to be Goliath

Open your Bible to 1 Samuel 17, and show the children the words.

say **Today's Bible story tells us that God can help us do great things.**

God's people were fighting a big strong army of people called Philistines. The Philistines had a huge soldier named Goliath. Have your "Goliath" step up on the stepstool, and let the children try to reach up to him.

Every day, Goliath would come out and say mean things about God's people.

ask • **When the Israelites heard mean Goliath, what do you think they did?**

say **They ran and hid! Even King Saul was afraid!** Have children run to the wall opposite where Goliath is standing and hide their eyes. **But there was one person who didn't run away. He wasn't big and strong. He wasn't even a soldier. His name was David, and he was just a boy. Get down and walk on your knees to show me how small David was.** Let children walk on their knees. **But little David wanted to fight big, scary Goliath. He knew that God would help him do great things.**

The king was surprised! David was so little, and Goliath was so big! David didn't even want to wear any armor or carry a spear. David knew that God could help him fight Goliath.

So David went to a stream and picked up one... (lead children in pretending to pick up stones as you slowly count) **two...three... four...five stones. Then he went to face Goliath.** Lead children to face Goliath. **David didn't need all five stones. He only needed one.** Have kids pretend to throw one stone at Goliath. **When that stone hit Goliath, he fell all the way to the ground.** Have your Goliath fall to the ground. Gather kids in a circle.

ask • **What great thing did God help David do?**

• **Why did God help David fight Goliath?**

• **What great things can God help you do?**

say You may not fight a big mean giant, but God can help you do great things. God loves us and wants us to try our best when we have to do something hard. With God's help, you can do things that seem too hard. If there's something God wants you to do, you can be sure that he'll help you!

BiBLe eXPeRiences

Bye-Bye Worries

Supplies: chalkboard and chalk or dry-erase white board and dry-erase markers

If your classroom doesn't have a chalkboard or dry-erase board, hang one sheet of construction paper per child and set out several crayons or markers.

Encourage children to stand at the board or at a sheet of paper. Have them each draw a picture of something that is scary or that worries them. After everyone has finished, tell the kids to pray and tell God their worry. When everyone has finished, have the kids either erase their picture or tear their picture down from the wall. If some of the kids are reluctant to erase their pictures or tear them from the wall, encourage them to draw a happy face on their pictures. Remind them that in today's Bible story they learned that if they tell God their worries, he will help them do great things.

- -

Giants and Small Guys

Supplies: large paper grocery sacks (1 per child), small paper lunch sacks (1 per child), markers or crayons, newspaper or scrap paper that can be crumpled, stapler

say In today's story, Goliath was much, much, much bigger than David, yet God was with David and helped him do great things. We are going to make a David and Goliath.

Give each child one large paper grocery sack and one small paper lunch sack. Have the children draw a Goliath face on the large sack and a David face on the small sack and then fill them with crumpled pieces of paper. Staple the tops of the sacks closed.

ask • Look how much bigger Goliath is; do you think David can beat Goliath all by himself?

• How did God help David beat Goliath?

say If we tell God our worries, then he will help us—even if our problems are great big!

Games

Stick to It!

Supplies: large paper with an outline of "Goliath" drawn on it, 1-inch dot stickers, tape

Tape the picture of Goliath to the wall so that his forehead can be reached by all the children. Give each child a 1-inch dot sticker.

say ▶ **Let's pretend these stickers are the stones that David used to fight Goliath.** Have children stand a few feet from the poster. Help one child spin several times in a circle. Remind the child that God helps us do everything. Instruct the child to close his or her eyes then try to put the "stone" on Goliath's forehead. Make sure every child has a turn.

ask ▶ • **Was it hard or easy to get the stone on Goliath?**

• **What things are hard for you to do?**

• **How do you feel knowing that God will help you do great things?**

say ▶ **Nobody believed that David could fight Goliath and win. But David did it because God helps us do great things. Even when things seem hard, remember to tell God your worries, and he will help you.**

Prayers

"God, You're Great!"

Supplies: none

Have kids stand in a circle and put their hands in the middle. Lead the children in the following prayer chant.

pray ▶ **God, you're great.**

Hear us chant and sing!

Thanks for helping us

Do great things.

Direct children to raise their hands and shout, "In Jesus' name, amen!"

snacks

Rock Cookies

Supplies: graham cracker crumbs, can of sweetened condensed milk, wax paper, chocolate chips

Before class, mix two cups of graham cracker crumbs and one can of sweetened condensed milk. Refrigerate the dough until class time.

Have the children wash their hands (or use wet wipes) then sit down to prepare their snack. Place a sheet of wax paper in front of each child. On each piece of wax paper, put five chocolate chips and a large spoonful of the dough mixture.

Say ▶ **Let's pretend the chocolate chips are the five stones that David picked up. You can use your dough to pick up the stones.**

Have children form their dough into the shape of a ball and then roll it on the chocolate chips so that the chips stick to the dough. This is a no-bake cookie, so kids can eat it as soon as you're ready!

ask ▶ • **How did it feel to make your own cookie?**

• **How do you think David felt when he won against Goliath?**

• **How can God help you do great things?**

Say ▶ **Let's thank God for helping us do great things and for providing our snack.** Invite one child to pray for the snack.

Songs

God Is Mighty

Supplies: none

Sing "God Is Mighty" to the tune of "Twinkle, Twinkle, Little Star." Encourage the kids to join you in repeating the words. Remind them that we can do mighty things because God is mighty and he helps us!

Sing ▶ **God is mighty.** *(Flex right arm.)*

God is strong. *(Flex left arm.)*

I will praise God all day long. *(Raise arms and stretch them out to the side.)*

God will help me do great things. *(Give two thumbs up.)*

That is why I praise and sing. *(Cup hands to mouth.)*

God is mighty. *(Flex right arm.)*

God is strong. *(Flex left arm.)*

I will praise God all day long. *(Raise arms and stretch them out to the side.)*

DAVID AND JONATHAN ARE FRIENDS

Bible Basis:

1 Samuel 18:1-4; 19:1-7; 20:1-42

Helping Each Other

Supplies: Bible, three arrows cut out of paper, pencils, tape

Before class, cut out three arrows, and tape each one on top of an unsharpened pencil. Then tip over a table to act as a rock that children will hide behind.

Open your Bible to 1 Samuel 18, and show the children the words.

say Today's Bible story tells us that friends help each other.

ask • Who are some of your good friends?

• What do you like to do with your friends?

say I'm so glad that you have friends. The Bible tells us that two boys named Jonathan and David were friends. Jonathan was King Saul's son, so he had a lot of really cool stuff. David's father was a shepherd, and he didn't have as much stuff. Friends help each other, so Jonathan shared his stuff with David.

Jonathan shared his sword. Let me see everyone pretend to wave a sword. Pause while children pretend. Jonathan shared his soldier uniform. Everyone pretend to put on a uniform. Pause and lead children in pretending. He shared his bow that he used to shoot arrows. Let me see everyone pretend to shoot a bow and arrow. Pause. And he shared his belt. Let's pretend to put on a belt. Pause.

King Saul got angry and wanted to hurt David. Jonathan wanted to help David because friends help each other. David went to hide behind a rock. Lead the children behind the overturned table to hide. Jonathan was very upset with King Saul. He didn't want his friend to get hurt, so he didn't tell King Saul where David was hiding. Jonathan made a special way to tell David if it was safe to come back. Jonathan had three arrows. Show children the "arrows," and let the children count them. If Jonathan shot the arrows over his servant's head, that meant that Jonathan was telling David to "go away, it's not safe here anymore." Move to the other side of the table. When the day came for Jonathan to send his message, this is what happened. Throw the three paper arrows over the children's heads. Let a child collect the arrows and give them to you.

ask · Since the arrows all went over your heads, what was the message?

say David knew he had to go away. David knew that friends help each other. David knew that it wasn't safe to be near King Saul, so he went away. David went away, but he was always ready to help Jonathan because friends help each other. Have children come back to the circle.

ask · How did Jonathan help David?

· How do you think Jonathan felt when he helped his friend?

· How do you feel when you help your friends?

say David and Jonathan were friends who helped each other just as you can help your friends. Friends help each other.

CRafts

Jonathan Sticks With David

Supplies: paper, corn syrup, water, food coloring, bowls, paintbrushes, measuring cup, toothpicks, wet wipes

Before class, mix 2/3 cup corn syrup and 1/3 cup water, then add a few drops of food coloring. Set out the paper, "paints," and paintbrushes, and let children each paint a picture of Jonathan and David. Talk about how sticky the paint is. Have wet wipes available for hand washing. Let each child set three toothpicks on his or her painting to represent arrows. The "arrows" will stick to the corn syrup paint.

ask · How did the paint feel?

· How did Jonathan help David?

· How can you stick with a friend and help him or her?

say Jonathan shot three arrows over David's head to tell him to go to a safe place. Friends help each other. The special paint on your paper feels very sticky, but when it dries it won't come off the paper, just as a friend will not leave you.

Sticking Close

Supplies: masking tape, paper plates, colored salt (salt can be colored by adding food coloring and stirring)

Tear pieces of masking tape long enough to fit around each child's wrist as a bracelet. Set out small plates of colored salt. You may want to set out confetti pieces as well. Have enough plates for one or two per child.

Put a tape bracelet on each child, sticky side out. Tell children that now they will try to be a friend who sticks closer than a brother. Let the children roll their wrists around on the plates of colored salt.

 • **What happened when you rolled your sticky bracelet in the salt?**

• **Can you tell me one way you could stick to a friend and help him or her?**

 Just like the salt stuck to the bracelet, friends can stick closer than a brother.

Games

Stuck Like Glue

Supplies: none

Gather children together in the center of the room.

 Today's Bible story was all about friends helping each other. Good friends stick together. Let's play a game about sticking to our friends! Choose one child to be the "Glue." **In this game, don't let the Glue tag you, or you'll be stuck to him [her]. If you're tagged, hold hands with the Glue and help tag others. We'll play until we're all stuck together!**

Start the game, and remind kids who are tagged to hold hands with the person who tagged them. Continue until everyone is stuck together. If time allows, play more rounds, choosing a different child each time to be the Glue.

 That was a fun game of getting all stuck together!

 • **How did the friends in today's Bible story stick together?**

• **How can you stick close and help a friend this week?**

Encourage children to follow through with their ideas for helping their friends. Then have a group hug.

PRAYERS

Happy to Help

Supplies: none

Have children sit in a circle. Let each child pray the following prayer, filling in a way that he or she could help a friend.

PRay ▶ **Dear God,**

Thank you for my friends. I want to help my friends by _____.

As each child prays, have him or her join hands with the child seated to the right. Make sure each child has a chance to pray and that all the kids are joining hands. **In Jesus' name, amen.**

Say ▶ **Now we are all stuck together like friends! This week, remember to help your friends because friends help each other.**

snacks

Helping Hands

Supplies: fruit leather, plastic knifes

Have the children wash their hands (or use wet wipes), then sit down to prepare their snack. Give each child a sheet of fruit leather, and have him or her unroll it. Have each child place one hand on the fruit leather while you trace his or her handprint with a plastic knife. (Some children may want to try this on their own.) Then let children pull their handprints from the fruit leather.

ask ▶ • **How did Jonathan use his hands to help David?**

• **How can you use your hands to help a friend?**

• **Why does God want us to help our friends?**

Say ▶ **Friends help each other as a way of showing God's love. You can help your friends by helping them clean up after playtime, tie their shoes, or even giving a hug! Let's thank God for helping Jonathan and David stick together and for providing our sticky snack.** Invite one child to pray for the snack.

Help, Help, Help Your Friends

Supplies: none

Gather in a circle, and sing "Help, Help, Help Your Friends" to the tune of "Row, Row, Row Your Boat." Encourage the kids to join you in repeating the verse.

SING **Help, help, help your friends, help them every day.**

Help them learn of Jesus' love

Through your helpful ways!

Encourage children to make up their own verses with ways they could help a friend.

Ten Little Friends

Supplies: none

Sing "Ten Little Friends" to the tune of "Ten Little Indians." Encourage the kids to join you in repeating the verse. Show children how to hold up their fingers and count the "friends" during the song. Remind them that God wants us to love our friends.

SING **One little, two little, three little friends,**

Four little, five little, six little friends,

Seven little, eight little, nine little friends,

Ten little friends praise God! *(Raise hands and wiggle fingers.)*

ELiJAH CHaLLenGes tHe PROPHets of BaaL

Bible Basis:

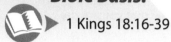

> 1 Kings 18:16-39

Supplies:

Bible, 2 candles, matches, red chenille wires

Open your Bible to 1 Kings 18, and show the children the words.

say **Today's Bible story tells us that we should serve God.**

The prophet Elijah gave special messages from God. Elijah found out that God's special people—the Israelites—forgot about God and started worshipping a fake god named Baal. Baal was just a silly statue! It would be ridiculous to worship and pray to a statue!

God wanted Elijah to prove to the people that God was real and Baal was fake. So God told Elijah to meet with all of Baal's people at a mountain for a showdown! Let's travel to the mountain and see what happens!

Have children follow you in a winding path around the room to your special story area. As you go, say things such as "This sure is a big mountain we're climbing" and "I wonder what that Elijah is up to." Gather children around the unlit candles.

say **Baal's people made an altar** (point to one candle)**, and Elijah made an altar** (point to the other candle)**. An altar in Bible times was like a stack of rocks and wood. It's a special place that helps people remember God. Elijah told the people, "You tell your god to send fire to your altar, then I'll ask my God to send fire to my altar. We'll see which god is real!"**

The people prayed to Baal and asked him to send fire on their altar. Nothing happened. Lead children in making a deep, bored sigh.

Then the people danced around their altar and asked Baal to send fire. Nothing happened. Have the children make a deeper, louder sigh.

Then they shouted, "Send fire, please!" What do you think happened? Pause. **Nothing happened. Baal wasn't real...so no fire came.** Lead children in another deep, loud sigh, then move one candle out of sight.

Next, it was Elijah's turn. Elijah had some men pour water all over the altar. Water doesn't burn! In fact, water is used to put out fires! Elijah was really going to show them that God was real. Then Elijah prayed to God. Have children fold their hands and repeat the following prayer after you: **Dear God, let these people know that you are the one and only God. Amen.**

ask · **What do you think happened?**

say **Elijah prayed and God answered.** Get out the matches, and light the candle. **God sent lots and lots of fire to the altar. In fact there was so much fire that it burned up the whole altar and all the water that had been poured on top!** Give each child one red chenille wire. Encourage them to form the wires into flames. Then have them wave their "flames." When the people saw the fire, they said, "The Lord—he is God!" Let's say that together. Lead children in cheering the phrase.

Collect the red chenille wires.

ask · **Which altar caught on fire?**

· **Who is the most powerful and one and only God?**

say **Elijah served the one true God and proved to everyone that Baal was fake. Jesus also taught us that we should serve God always. Jesus said to serve God in everything we do. That means we should serve God when we are eating, when we are playing, even when we are brushing our teeth! We can serve God all the time by praying to him, praising him with music, or giving him our love. Just like Elijah, we should serve God only.**

Blow out the candle.

Elijah's Altar

Supplies: brown paper lunch sacks, red or yellow chenille wires, brown and gray crayons or markers, red or yellow tissue paper, scissors

Set out brown paper lunch sacks, red or yellow chenille wires, brown and gray crayons or markers, and red or yellow tissue paper.

Encourage the children to use the gray and brown markers to draw stones and logs on their brown paper lunch sacks. Then show the children how to crumple their bags. Once the children have finished coloring and crumpling their sacks, walk around and cut a 3x2-inch slit in the bottom of each bag. Direct the children to tear out a "flame" from the red or yellow tissue paper. Instruct the children to wrap the chenille wire around the tissue paper, so the "flame" is on a stick. Then have them insert the flame stick through the open side of the bag into the slit at the bottom.

say **Let's pretend we are at the altar with Elijah and act out the story we heard today using our pretend flames. When the people shout to Baal, keep the flame hidden, but when Elijah prays, push up your flame and say: "Serve God only."** Lead children in pushing their flames up and down in their paper bags as you "call on" either God or Baal.

ask **• How did the people in today's Bible story know that God was the true God?**

• What are some ways that we know God is the true God?

say **In today's Bible story, God brought fire and Baal didn't. Sometimes in our own lives, God does powerful things like make snow or beautiful sunsets. God is all around us, and we know that he is the one and only true God!**

No Other Gods

Supplies: none

Lead children in a game similar to London Bridge. Choose two children to join hands overhead and make a bridge. Lead the other children in walking under the bridge singing "No Other Gods" to the tune of "London Bridge."

sing → **We will serve no other gods,**

Other gods,

Other gods.

We will serve no other gods.

Serve God only!

On the last line, have the "bridge" lower its arms to trap one child. Ask that child the following question.

ask → **• How can you show that God is important?**

Then let the child become half of the bridge. Play until everyone has had a turn to be "caught."

say → **God wants us to serve him only. In the Bible God says, "You must not have any other god but me." That means that we put God first in everything we do!**

PRayeRS

Action Prayer

Supplies: paper cross, washable ink pad, wet wipes, tape

Have children sit in a circle.

 Elijah showed the people that God was the one true God. Hold up one finger to show that you believe God is the one true God. Pause. **Let's use our fingers to show that we serve God by praying.**

Set out the ink pad and let children each take turns pressing a finger on the ink pad then making one fingerprint on the paper cross. As children each make a fingerprint, have them say, "God, I will serve you." Provide wet wipes for children to clean their fingers.

 God, we want to serve you in all we do. Help us to be like Elijah and show everyone that you are the one true God. In Jesus' name, amen.

Tape the paper cross on your classroom door to show everyone that the children know God is the one true God.

Snacks

Here Comes the Fire!

Supplies: napkins, crackers, shredded cheddar cheese

Have children wash their hands (or use wet wipes) then sit down to prepare their snacks. Set out crackers, shredded cheddar cheese, and napkins.

Let children make "altars" by stacking three or four crackers.

ask • **What happened to Baal's altar?**

say **Nothing happened to it, because Baal was a fake! Praying to a fake god is sort of like asking a chair to do something! That was foolish.**

ask • **After Elijah prayed, what happened to his altar?**

say **God sent down fire to prove he was the one and only true God. God wants us to serve only him and not any fake gods!**

Ask a volunteer to pray for the snack, thanking God for being real and powerful. Then let children add shredded cheese "flames" to the top of their altars.

"Serve God" Rhyme

Supplies: none

As you teach your children this rhyme, remind them to serve God always.

 One, two. *(Hold up one finger, then two.)*

God is true. *(Give two thumbs up.)*

Two, three. *(Hold up two fingers, then three.)*

God loves me! *(Point to self.)*

Three, four. *(Hold up three fingers, then four.)*

Serve the Lord. *(Point up.)*

Four, five. *(Hold up four fingers, then five.)*

God's alive! *(Jump up and raise fists in the air.)*

ELISHA HELPS A WIDOW AND HER SONS

Bible Basis:

> 2 Kings 4:1-7

Supplies:

Bible, small amount of colored water in a clear pitcher, paper cups, tarp, chalkboard and chalk or paper and marker, large pitcher full of colored water

Before class, hide paper cups around the room.

Open your Bible to 2 Kings 4, and show children the words.

say **Today's Bible story tells us that God cares for people in need.**

The Bible tells us about a widow who lived with her two sons. Her husband had died, and she owed people money, but she had no money to pay the people back. Direct the kids to check their pockets for money. **She didn't even have food to eat for the next week, so she asked Elisha for help. Elisha was a prophet—he gave people messages from God.**

ask • **When have you needed help?**

• **Who did you go to for help?**

say **The widow asked Elisha for help, and Elisha asked the woman what she had in her house and how he could help her. She told him that all she had left that was worth any money was a little bit of oil in a jar. We'll pretend that this colored water is the little bit of oil that the widow had.** Hold up the pitcher that has the small amount of colored water. **Elisha told the widow to go to all of her neighbors and ask to borrow lots and lots of empty jars. Let's pretend to be the woman looking for jars, and let's look around our room for empty paper cups.** Help the children find all of the hidden cups, then have the children sit down in a circle on the tarp.

After the widow collected lots of jars, Elisha told her to take her small jar of oil and pour oil into the borrowed jars.

Hold up the pitcher of water with just a small amount of water in it. Ask the children to guess how many of the cups you'll be able to fill with just the little bit of "oil," and write the numbers on a piece of paper or on a chalkboard. Then fill the cups with what you have in your pitcher. (You should be able to fill only two or three small cups.) Compare the actual results with the estimates.

say ▶ Hmmm. It looks like we could use some more "oil"—I'd like to be able to fill all of our cups, just like in the Bible story.

Have a volunteer bring in the large pitcher of colored water, and have him or her say, "It looks like you have some more cups to fill. Let me take care of you like God took care of the widow!" Then ask the children to estimate how many more cups can be filled with the liquid in the large pitcher of "oil." Pour the liquid into all of the remaining paper cups. Try to make sure you have enough water to fill all of the cups (just like in the Bible story). Have the kids thank the volunteer for his or her help.

ask ▶ • How did you feel when we didn't have enough "oil"?

• How did you feel when more "oil" was given to us?

say ▶ Just like [name of volunteer] took care of us and brought us more "oil," God did a miracle and helped the widow! She had just a little bit of oil to start with, but God gave the widow enough oil to fill all of the jars! Elisha then told the woman to sell the oil and use the money to pay back the people she owed money to. She even had enough left over to buy food for herself and her sons. God cares for people in need, and God sent Elisha to help the widow and her sons.

ask ▶ • How do you think the widow felt after God sent Elisha to help her?

• How has God helped you when you've needed something?

say ▶ God helped the widow and her sons when they were in need. God helps us, too. We may be sad and need some comfort, or be hungry and need something to eat, or be lonely and need a friend. God gives us people who love and care for us—God cares for people in need. Let the kids come up one at a time and help pour the liquid back into the pitchers as they repeat "God cares for people in need."

Just as God cared for the widow and her sons, Jesus also cared for people in need when he was on earth. Jesus healed people who were sick, he gave comfort and love to people who were sad or broken on the inside, and Jesus died for all of us so that we would be forgiven for all of the bad things we do. Jesus cared for people in need when he was on earth, and Jesus is still caring for you! Jesus loves you and wants you to care for people in need just as he did.

Bible Experiences

Fill My Jars

Supplies: cups, bowls, water

Let the children experiment with water in the cups and bowls. Encourage your children to count how many small cups it takes to fill one big bowl. Remind kids that God cares for people in need.

ask ▸ • How do you think the widow felt when she was told to fill all of the jars with her little bit of oil?

say ▸ God loves all of us very much. He was the one who made it possible for the woman to fill her jars when she only had a tiny bit of oil.

Caring Collage

Supplies: glue sticks, children's magazines, sheets of construction paper cut into heart shapes

Set out a supply of glue sticks and age-appropriate magazines. Give children each a piece of construction paper already cut into a heart shape. Tell children they are going to pretend that the heart shape is God's heart, and they are going to fill God's heart with pictures of people God loves. Show children how to tear out pictures of people from magazines and glue the pictures on the heart shape to make a collage. Tell kids that today's Bible story is about a family who needed help and that God sent someone to help the family. On each child's collage, write, "God cares for people in need." Say the words aloud as you write on each child's paper. Remind children that God cares for people in need because God loves the people.

Care Share

Supplies: stickers

Tell children that God loves it when people care for each other. Caring for others is a way to share God's love. Give each child two stickers. Tell children that they can each keep one of their stickers; it's a gift from you because you love and care for them. Then tell kids that the other sticker is for them to give to someone else. Encourage each child to keep the extra sticker in a pocket until he or she decides to give it to someone. Tell kids that they can use their extra stickers to show care to people they know. Remind kids that God wants us to care for others, just as he cared for the widow and her sons.

Thanks for Caring!

Supplies: sheet of poster board, crayons or markers

Invite your children to think of the people in your community who help others in need. Kids might suggest doctors, nurses, firefighters, paramedics, or police officers. Have children decide together which of these service groups they'd like to send a big thank-you card to.

Then set out a large sheet of poster board, and let everyone contribute to the class card. Kids can draw pictures of themselves, make handprints, draw hearts, or write their names on the poster board. At the top of the poster, write "Thank you!" in big letters. Tell children you'll deliver the class card during the coming week. (Make sure you remember to do so!) Remind kids that God takes care of everyone in need.

Oil Painting

Supplies: paper with a jar drawn on it (create one "original" and make one copy for each child), sponges or cotton balls soaked in oil

Give each child a picture of the jar. Remind kids that the widow in today's Bible lesson had only one jar of oil when Elisha came to visit her. Have the kids hold up one finger.

say ▶ **One jar of oil is not very much. The widow would have run out soon, but God cared for her by filling lots and lots of other jars from just that one jar. Let's take one finger and make some tiny jars of oil to remind us of the way God cared for the widow.**

Encourage kids to each press one finger onto the sponge or cotton ball and then press their finger onto the jar on their papers. Have kids make several small "jars" on their papers.

say ▶ **Our fingerprints look like tiny jars of oil.** Encourage children to share how many fingerprint jars they made on their paper. **God helped Elisha and the widow fill jar after jar with oil. One jar of oil filled many, many other jars—and the first jar was still full! Only God can do something like that!**

Have kids hold their pictures up to the light. Point out that the jar looks like it is filled with oil.

ask ▶ • **Have you ever run out of something? What did you do?**

• **How has God provided for your family?**

say ▶ **God cared for the widow in a special way. God cares for us in special ways, too. God knows what we need, and he has promised to take care of us. God cares for people in need.**

PRAYERS

World Prayer

Supplies: a world globe

 say God cares for people in need, and he loves people all over the world.

Have the kids pass around the globe and take turns saying the names of people God loves, such as their moms or dads, relatives, siblings, or friends. Then close by having the children repeat each line of the following prayer after you.

PRay Dear God,

Thank you for caring for people in need.

Thank you for loving the people from all over the world.

Thank you for your love, protection, and care for all of us.

In Jesus' name, amen.

SNACKS

Bread and Oil

Supplies: paper plates (coated plates work better than plain ones), oil, shredded parmesan cheese, salt, various dried herbs, bread

Have children wash their hands (or use wet wipes) and then gather to make their snack. Choose a child to pray and thank God for giving them the snack they need today.

Then give each child a plate with a few tablespoons of oil on it. Let the children add pinches of cheese, salt, and herbs to make a dipping sauce. Show the children how to dip their bread into the oil and taste it. Remind the children that God gave the woman the oil she needed for her family.

ask • How can you thank God for giving you all of this oil?

• When we have a need, can we trust God to help us? Why?

say God knows exactly what we need, and he makes sure that we have what we need. God cares for people in need.

SONGS

"God Cares for You" Rhyme

Supplies: none

As you teach the children this action rhyme, remind them that God cares for people in need.

 No matter where you live *(touch your fingertips over your head to make a "roof")*
Or where you go *(march in place),*
God cares for you. *(Place hands over heart.)*
His love he will show. *(Open arms wide.)*

Our God Cares

Supplies: none

Lead the children in singing "Our God Cares" to the tune of "She'll Be Coming Round the Mountain." Encourage the kids to join you in singing and doing the motions.

 Oh, our God cares for people *(hug someone)*
When they're in need.
Oh, our God cares for people *(give someone a high five)*
When they're in need.
Our God cares for people. *(Pat someone's back.)*
Our God cares for people.
Oh, our God cares for people *(shake someone's hand)*
When they're in need.

God Will Take Good Care of You

Supplies: none

Lead the children in singing "God Will Take Good Care of You" to the tune of "Mary Had a Little Lamb." Encourage kids to join in the motions.

 God will take good care of you *(point up),*
Care of you *(point at someone else),*
Care of you. *(Point at someone else.)*
God will take good care of you. *(Point up.)*
The Bible says it's true. *(Hold your hands in front of you like a book.)*

God will take good care of me *(point up),*
Care of me *(point at yourself),*
Care of me. *(Point at yourself.)*
God will take good care of me. *(Point up.)*
This I do believe. *(Point to your temple.)*

JOSIAH DISCOVERS GOD'S WORD

Bible Basis:

> 2 Chronicles 34:1-33

Supplies:

Bible, gingerbread-man paper figures, blocks, paintbrushes

Before you begin the Bible story, tell the kids to strap on imaginary tool belts because they're going to be King Josiah's workers in the story. Then open your Bible to 2 Chronicles 34, and show children the words.

say ▸ **Today's Bible story tells us that God's Word is important.**

Read the following story, and lead the "workers" in their parts.

say ▸ **Josiah was only 8 years old when he became king. That's only a few years older than you are now! Josiah was a good king who obeyed God. When Josiah grew up, he became a great king who obeyed and loved God.**

ask ▸ **· How can we obey God?**

say ▸ **We obey God when we** [say some of the things the kids shared] **and when we do what the Bible tells us to do. God's Word is important!**

King Josiah saw that there were lots of idols in his kingdom. Idols are statues that people worship. Let's pretend that these paper figures are the idols that the people were worshipping. Place the paper figures in the center of your circle. **The people thought that the idols were more important than God. So King Josiah called all his workers together.** Have kids stand at attention in a straight line and salute.

"We must get rid of all these bad idols!" King Josiah told the workers. "Smash them, crash them, smush them, crush them!" he called out. Have the kids each take a paper doll and tear it up as they repeat the words: "Smash them, crash them, smush them, crush them."

"Stomp them, tromp them—God doesn't want them!" Have the kids stomp their feet as they say, "Stomp them, tromp them—God doesn't want them."

So King Josiah and his workers got rid of the idols. When that was done, King Josiah needed his workers for another job. Have the kids stand at attention and salute. **Parts of God's Temple, or church, were**

old and broken and cracked. So Josiah called for his workers. But this time he wanted them to build—not to tear down.

"Hammer up that board; we'll fix it for the Lord!" Josiah said. Have the kids pretend to hammer on the blocks as they build the Temple wall and say the words: "Hammer up that board; we'll fix it for the Lord!"

"Let's sweep and brush and get rid of this dust!" Have the children pretend to sweep with a paintbrush as they repeat the sentence: "Let's sweep and brush and get rid of this dust!"

While the workers were busy fixing up the Temple, the priest found something very important. It was the Book of the Law of God, which had been lost and forgotten for many years.

ask • **Have you ever found something that you thought was lost? How did you feel when you found it?**

Bring out the Bible, and pass it around to the kids. As each child holds the Bible, have him or her say, "God's Word is important."

say **The priest took the book to King Josiah. When Josiah heard the words in the book, he said, "We must follow these laws and do what God wants." King Josiah called together all of the people in his kingdom: the rich, the poor, his helpers—everyone.** Have the kids form a circle around you as you hold the Bible. **King Josiah read God's Word to them and said, "This book is so important. I promise to follow God and keep his commands. Who else will also promise to follow God?" And all of the people said, "We promise."** Have the children raise their hands and say, "We promise to follow God." **All of the people followed God, and that pleased God.** Have the kids sit in a circle. **God's Word was important to King Josiah.**

ask • **Why do you think God's Word, the Bible, is so important?**

• **What did Josiah promise to do?**

say **God's Word is so important! King Josiah and all of the people promised to follow God all of their lives. Let's promise to follow God's Word, because it tells us about God's love and it shows us how to live. The Bible also tells us about Jesus. It tells us about Jesus' life and that Jesus came to earth to help us live forever. We can read all about Jesus in the Bible. The stories about Jesus are back here, after the story about Josiah.** Show kids where the New Testament is. **Let's tell everyone we meet to follow God's Word, just as Josiah did!**

BiBLe eXPeRieNceS

Directions for Life

Supplies: Bible, balsa wood toy glider

Have the children form a circle and sit down, then bring out the glider parts.

say ▶ **Hmmm…I wonder what this bunch of stuff will be when it's put together.** Let the kids guess as you make a big show of trying to put the glider together—and not getting it right.

ask ▶ **• What would help me know how to put this together?**

Wait for kids to say "directions," then bring out the directions. Read each step aloud, and have a couple of volunteers help you put the glider together. Hold up the completed glider bird.

say ▶ **I wondered what those pieces were going to be, and I even worried a bit, but I didn't need to. There were directions all the time. The directions were good, and they helped us put together the glider. It's great!**

Pass the glider around the circle and let each child inspect it. As the kids play with the glider, continue your discussion.

say ▶ **King Josiah was worried about his people and his kingdom. He didn't know how to make his people obey God and stop bowing down to idols.** Hold up a Bible. **When King Josiah found God's Word, he realized that God's Word is like directions and could help him put together his kingdom right, just as the directions helped us put together the glider bird. God was happy that King Josiah promised to follow God's Word and the directions in it. God's Word is important.**

ask ▶ **• How is God's Word like directions?**

• How can you follow the directions in God's Word?

say ▶ **God's Word is important. We can follow the directions in God's Word to help us do what is right.**

Today we learned that God's Word is important. I'd like each of you to choose a way you'll use God's Word this week.

Give kids these three ideas to choose from:

• Have your mom or dad read you a Bible story.

• Act out a Bible story with your brother or sister or with a friend.

- **Call your grandma or grandpa, and tell her or him your favorite Bible story.**

Allow the kids to either choose from these three ideas or take a minute to think of a few new ideas together. Then have the kids turn to a partner nearby and tell the partner which idea they've chosen. Make sure you choose an idea as well, and tell a partner. Your commitment will inspire your children and will give them an opportunity to see God at work in your life as well as theirs!

CRafts

A Book by Any Other Name

Supplies: stickers, paper, crayons

Give each child two stickers, a sheet of paper, and crayons. Have children place their stickers on the paper and then "write" on it with the crayons. Then help children roll up the papers and seal them with stickers to create scrolls like the ones found during Josiah's reign.

say ▶ **When Josiah was king, God's Word was written on paper and then rolled up. Today, the Bible contains God's Word, and it's important to us because it tells how God wants us to live. Even though the scroll from Josiah's day and our Bible today look different on the outside, both have God's Word on the inside. God's Word is important because it tells everyone, even children, how to make good choices and live for God.**

ask ▶ **• Why is God's Word important?**

say ▶ **Josiah knew that God's Word was important. He wanted the people to listen to God's Word. We must listen to it, too. God's Word is important.**

Hot and Cold Bible Hunt

Supplies: Bible

Encourage children to join in this game of Hot and Cold Bible Hunt. Have all the children close their eyes, and then hide a Bible so that it cannot be seen. Once it is hidden, have the children open their eyes and begin looking. If they are close to where the Bible is, say "hot." If they are far from where the Bible is, say "cold." If they are somewhere in between but getting closer, say, "You're getting warmer." If they are getting farther away, say, "You're getting colder."

Once the Bible is found, you can play again if there is time. Use this time to affirm the children by saying things like "You are doing a really good job of listening to my clues," or "Wow, you found the Bible very quickly." Remind kids that in today's story they heard about some workers who were cleaning the Temple and found God's Word.

Follow the Leader

Supplies: none

Play a game of Follow the Leader. Give each child a turn to be the Leader and lead the other kids in doing fun motions and silly movements. Remind children that King Josiah taught his people to follow God, the very best leader of all.

Prayers

Singing Prayer

Supplies: none

Go around the circle and have the kids each tell when a parent or older sibling might read them a story from God's Word this week. For example, a child might have a parent read a Bible story at bedtime each night. Then close by singing this prayer.

Lead the kids in singing "God, We Thank You" to the tune of "Jesus Loves Me." Have the children hold their hands side by side as if they're holding a Bible.

SING   **God, we thank you for your book;**

Every day we'll take a look!

The Bible tells us what is true;

It helps us to follow you.

Yes, we will follow;

Yes, we will follow;

Yes, we will follow

Your important words.

Have the children close by saying together, "In Jesus' name, amen."

snacks

Royal Roll-ups

Supplies: paper plates, napkins, plastic knives, tortillas, softened cream cheese, raisins

Have the children wash their hands before they prepare the snacks. Give each child a napkin, a paper plate, a tortilla, and a plastic knife. Allow the children to spread a thin layer of cream cheese on their tortillas, then let the kids use the raisins to form the first letter of their names. Or you could write words such as "God," "love," or "Bible" on a chalkboard or white board for the kids to copy.

Explain to the children that the important book the priest found probably looked more like a scroll. Demonstrate how to carefully lift up one end of a tortilla and roll it up.

say   **God loves us so much that he gave us a very special and important book—the Bible. God gave us the Bible so we could have everything we need to help him. It makes God very happy when we follow his Word and tell others about God. God's Word is important.**

Invite a child to pray. Then have kids share ideas on how we help God such as by telling others about God, bringing friends to church, or helping friends learn to love God.

A Palatable Page

Supplies: paper plates, plastic knives, graham crackers, cream cheese frosting, decorator icing

Have children wash their hands (or use wet wipes). Then gather the children around a table. Give each child a paper plate, a plastic knife, and a graham cracker square. Tell the children that they are going to make Bible pages. Have children use the plastic knives to spread cream cheese frosting onto the graham crackers. Then have kids pretend to write words with decorator icing. Remind children that God's Word is important because we can learn how to live for God by reading his Word. Pray to thank God for the Bible, and then let children eat the "pages."

 ask
- **Why is God's Word important?**
- **What is your favorite Bible story?**

say **We can read God's Word and learn more about God and Jesus. God's Word is important!**

 SONGS

God Spoke His Word

Supplies: none

As you teach the children this active rhyme, show them how to do a simple clapping rhythm as you say the words below by slapping their knees once and then clapping their hands once.

RHYME **God spoke his Word so we could know**

About the way he loves us so.

It's written in his book so dear,

Important words that we must hear.

Read God's Word

Supplies: none

Lead the children in singing "Read God's Word" to the tune of "The Mulberry Bush."

SING **Find someone to read God's Word,**
Read God's Word, read God's Word.
Find someone to read God's Word
Each and every day.

Listen and obey God's Word,
Obey God's Word, obey God's Word.
Listen and obey God's Word
Each and every day.

NeHeMiaH ReBuiLDS tHe WaLL

Bible Basis:

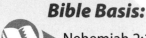 Nehemiah 2:11–6:19

Supplies:

Bible, blocks in several piles

Gather the kids near the piles of blocks. Open your Bible to Nehemiah 2, and show the children the words.

say ▸ **Today's Bible story tells us to work hard for God.**

Nehemiah was worried about the people and sad that the wall of the city was broken down. Point to the blocks on the floor. **Nehemiah turned to God for help. God answered Nehemiah's prayers, and the king allowed Nehemiah to go to Jerusalem to help rebuild the city wall.**

Nehemiah and his friends worked hard for God as they rebuilt the city wall. Let's pretend that we're working with Nehemiah and the people. Let's turn this jumble of blocks into a nice, strong wall.

Encourage kids to use the blocks to build a very tall wall.

ask ▸ **• When you saw all of these piles, how did you feel about working to build them into a wall?**

• When Nehemiah and God's people saw the broken-down city wall, how do you think they felt about working to build the wall back up again?

say ▸ **The people may have thought, "Oh, what a lot of work!" But they must have been excited, too, to finally rebuild their city. They worked hard for God as they finished the wall.**

ask ▸ **• What do you think of your finished work with these blocks?**

• How can you work hard for God?

say ▸ **Nehemiah and God's people celebrated when they finished building. Our wall looks great, too! Whether we're building a wall or doing chores at home or helping a neighbor do yardwork, we can learn from Nehemiah to work hard for God.**

We can also learn from Jesus how to work hard for God. When Jesus was on earth, he did hard and wonderful work for God. Jesus traveled all over the land to tell others about God. Jesus healed people, and he prayed for people. Jesus loved God, and he wanted to work hard for God. We can work hard for God just like Nehemiah and Jesus.

Lead everyone in clapping and cheering for their well-built wall!

BiBLe eXPeRieNCeS

The City Walls

Supplies: paper, crayons or markers, squares of paper that resemble blocks, glue

Distribute the paper, and have the kids write their names on them. Direct the children to the paper "blocks," and have the children glue the blocks to the paper to represent helping Nehemiah rebuild the wall. Remind the children that Nehemiah worked hard for God, and we can work hard for God, too.

ask • How did Nehemiah work hard for God in our Bible story?

• What are ways you can work hard for God?

say Nehemiah worked hard for God when he helped God's people rebuild the city wall. We can work hard for God, too. In everything we do, we can work as though we're working for God!

Work on the Wall

Supplies: city drawings (draw a simple ancient city on a piece of paper and photocopy one for each child), glue, brown paper cut into strips

Distribute city drawings, and write children's names on them. Give kids glue and brown paper strips. Encourage kids to glue their strips onto their pages to help rebuild the wall in front of the city. Ask the following questions as the children work hard to build walls.

ask • **How do you think the people felt when they helped repair the city wall?**

• **What jobs have you worked hard to finish?**

• **How do you think God feels when we work hard for him?**

say **We can work hard for God when we work on any project. God wants us to help each other by working hard for him.**

Helpful Hammers

Supplies: glue sticks, wrapping paper scraps, paper hammers (create a large hammer outline on a piece of paper; copy and cut out one per child)

Set out the glue sticks and the wrapping paper scraps. Give each child a paper hammer. Have kids glue the wrapping paper scraps onto their hammers. Encourage kids to make collages by overlapping the edges of the wrapping paper and filling in the empty spaces until one side of each hammer is completely covered. Ask children to each think of one job they can do this week to help someone else. Encourage each child to draw a picture of something that would remind him or her of that activity on the blank side of the hammer.

ask • **How do we know when we are being helpful?**

• **What are some ways you can be helpful this week?**

say **God sees everything we do. When we help others, it's like helping God. We can work hard for God by helping others. These hammers will remind you that whenever you work hard for God, it's like giving God a special gift!**

Prayer Builders

Supplies: none

Ask the children to stand up and make a human wall by linking their arms together at their elbows. Say this prayer, and have the children repeat it after you one line at a time.

PRay **Dear God,**
Here we stand, oh so tall,
Connected like a mighty wall.
Help us work hard just for you
Every day, in all we do!
In Jesus' name, amen.

Action Prayer

Supplies: a brick

Ask the children to come stand around a brick laid on a table.

say **Today we learned about Nehemiah, who worked hard for God. Let's place our hands on this brick and tell God that we want to work hard for him.** Have the children take turns placing their hands on the brick and praying the following prayer.

PRay **Dear God, help me to work hard for you. In Jesus' name, amen.**

Wall of Protection

Supplies: graham crackers, craft sticks, paper plates, cream cheese

Have children wash their hands (or use wet wipes). Give each child at least four small graham crackers and a craft stick on a plate. Tell the children that they will build walls to help make their city look nice and to keep the people and animals safe. Have each child put a small dab of cream cheese on the craft stick and then rub the cream cheese onto the short ends of the graham cracker. Have children stick the crackers together to build the city walls. Remind the children that they are working hard for God to build their walls, just as Nehemiah and his friends worked hard for God.

ask · **How did it feel to work hard to make your wall?**

· **How do you think Nehemiah felt as he worked hard for God?**

say **We all worked hard for God and got the job done. Let's give ourselves a hand for our good work!** Choose a child to thank God for today's snack, and then let kids enjoy eating it.

Edible Bricks

Supplies: bowl, spoon, can of frosting, 2 cups of powdered sugar, wax paper, shredded coconut

Have kids create small bricks for a snack. Before class, mix a can of frosting and two cups of powdered sugar to make dough. Stir the dough until it is the consistency of modeling clay, adding more powdered sugar if necessary.

Have children wash their hands (or use wet wipes). Give each child a sheet of wax paper and some coconut. Sprinkle powdered sugar on the wax paper to keep the frosting mixture from sticking. Give each child about one tablespoon of the mixture, and explain that when the Israelites saw the broken wall, they knew they would have to make bricks of clay and straw to fix it. Show the children how to make rectangular bricks by using the mix as clay and the coconut as straw. Allow each child to eat a "brick" for his or her snack.

SONGS

"Work Hard Everywhere" Rhyme

Supplies: none

Children love to act out how they see adults working. Let this rhyme reinforce that preschoolers can also work hard for God. Ask the children to stand up and follow you in the motions as you teach them this rhyme about working for God.

 Do your work with all your heart *(make a pounding motion with one fist)*

At home, at church, at school. *(Turn to the left, turn to the right, then touch the ground.)*

Jump right in, and do your part. *(Jump forward.)*

Working hard for God is cool! *(Give a thumbs-up sign.)*

Work for God

Supplies: none

Lead the children in walking in a circle as you sing "Work for God" to the tune of "Mary Had a Little Lamb."

 Yes, I will work hard for God,
Work for God, work for God.
Yes, I will work hard for God
Each and every day.

Daniel is Safe in the Lions' Den

Bible Basis:

 Daniel 6:1-23

Supplies:

Bible, paper plates, crayons or markers, washable ink pad, blank poster board, wet wipes

Open your Bible to Daniel 6, and show the children the words. Give each child a paper plate, and set out crayons or markers.

Say **Today's Bible story tells us that God takes care of us.**

Before we begin today's Bible story, I want each of you to imagine the biggest, meanest, hungriest lion you can think of. Got it? Now draw the face of that lion on your paper plate the best that you can. As the kids are drawing their lions, briefly tell them the first part of the story:

We're drawing lions today because that's what today's story is about—God took care of Daniel when Daniel was thrown into a den with some mean, hungry lions!

Daniel didn't do anything wrong to get in trouble. In fact, it was because he did everything right! Everybody say, "Daniel loved God." Pause for the kids to repeat the sentence. **Everybody knew that Daniel loved God—even the king. Daniel was special, and the king gave Daniel an important job. But the rest of the king's men said, "The king is a fool! Daniel can't rule!"** Lead the children in repeating the words.

So the king's men came up with a plan. They had the king agree that everyone should pray to the king, not to God. If anyone broke that rule, they'd be thrown into the lions' den. Everyone say, "Oh, my!" Pause while the children respond.

Was Daniel worried? Not a bit. He knew that God takes care of us. Daniel prayed to God just as he always did. This time when the king's men were spying on Daniel, they caught him breaking the new rule.

The king's men told the king that Daniel was praying to God. The king was very sad to hear this news, because Daniel was special. But a rule's a rule! There was no way that the king could take back his rule. Daniel had to be thrown in with the hungry lions.

Have kids hold up their lion faces and pretend to growl at Daniel.

say **When Daniel was thrown in with the hungry lions, God caused the lions' mouths to stay shut so they didn't hurt Daniel! Everyone put down your lion faces and shout, "Yea, Daniel!"** Pause as everyone responds. **The king was sad that he had to throw Daniel in with the lions, so he came to check on Daniel. When he found out that Daniel was OK, the king was excited, too! Everyone say, "Yea, Daniel!" again.** Pause as kids respond.

ask • **How do you think Daniel felt when he was thrown in with the hungry lions?**

• **How did God take care of Daniel in the lions' den?**

• **How would you want God to take care of you?**

say **Let's draw the ways that you want God to take care of you on this poster.** Encourage each child to use a crayon or marker to draw on the poster board his or her answer to the question "How would you want God to take care of you?"

God takes care of us, just like he took care of Daniel! Whenever we feel afraid or worried, all we have to do is pray to God and tell him about our problems, and God will always take care of us in the way that's best! Let's put a handprint beside our pictures to show that we can fold our hands and pray for God to take care of us. Have kids press one hand onto an ink pad and then press the same hand on or beside their picture on the poster. Use wet wipes or wet paper towels to clean kids' hands after they have stamped their handprint.

When Jesus was on earth, he trusted God to take care of him, too. Jesus prayed that God would be with him and that God would do the very best thing for him and for all the people in the world. Jesus loved the people of the world so much that he died on the cross so that everyone could go to heaven and be with God. God took care of Jesus though, and Jesus came back to life after three days! God loved Jesus and took care of him, and God loves us and will take care of us!

BiBLe eXPeRieNCeS

Care Pairs

Supplies: stuffed animals (1 for each pair of children), a variety of pet care supplies, ribbons, gift bows

Have the children form pairs. Give each pair a stuffed animal, and talk about the things that people need to do to care for their pets. Let the partners work together to brush, feed, walk, and find other ways to care for their stuffed animals. Let the children use bows and ribbons to make their pets beautiful. Line up a row of chairs, and have the children place their animals on the chairs for a pet show. Give a gift bow to each stuffed animal for "best-cared-for pet."

 • **What are some things that you and your partner did to take care of your toy pet?**

• **Who has God given you to take care of you?**

 When we take care of our real pets or our stuffed animals, we learn what it means to love something and take care of something. God gives us family and friends who care for us. God loves us, and God takes care of us!

Tail Tale

Supplies: four 24-inch strips of raffia or yarn per child, 2 rubber bands per child, safety pins

Before class, make a lion's tail for each child by folding four 24-inch strips of raffia (or yarn) in half and securing with a rubber band one inch from the fold. Add another rubber band four inches from the end of the raffia strips to make the tassel of the lion's tail. Give each child a tail, and let children pretend to be lions. Place a safety pin through the folded end of the tail, and attach it to the back of each child at his or her waist. Remind children that in today's story God saved Daniel from being eaten by lions.

CRAFTS

In the Lions' Den

Supplies: paper, markers, muffin tin liners, glue sticks

Distribute sheets of paper, and have the kids write their names on them. Encourage the children each to glue a muffin tin liner "head" onto the paper and draw a lion's body on the page. Let the kids draw lions' faces inside the liners and draw an X over the lions' mouths.

ask • How did God take care of Daniel when Daniel was in the lions' den?

• How has God taken care of you when you've been worried or afraid?

say God takes care of us no matter what we're going through. We can tell God our worries and trust that he'll take care of us. When we show others that we trust in God, they'll know that God will take care of them, too!

Lions' Den

Supplies: paper plates, modeling dough, drinking straws, markers, craft sticks, pompoms

Give each child a paper plate. Have kids each roll 10 walnut-size balls out of modeling dough and place the balls in a circle on their plate. Encourage kids to stick one drinking straw into each modeling-dough ball to form a cage-like den. Have each child use markers to draw a face on his or her craft stick. Finally, have children each put in their den two or three pompoms to represent the lions and the craft stick to represent Daniel. Encourage children to spend a few minutes retelling the story using their craft. Tell kids that they can take their craft home and use it to tell the story of Daniel to their family and friends.

ask • Why wasn't Daniel afraid when he was in the lions' den?

• Why should we trust God when we are in scary situations?

say No matter how scary a situation might seem, we know that God loves us and wants what is best for us. God takes care of us.

A Strutting Song

Supplies: bedsheet

Set two to four chairs several feet apart, and spread a bedsheet across the top of them to create a "lions' den." Let the children pretend to be lions crawling on all fours. Encourage them to enter the lions' den and roar, stretch themselves importantly, and strut around.

As children act like lions, encourage them to sing "The Lion Strut" to the tune of "Row, Row, Row Your Boat." Explain to children that the word "strut" means to walk around proudly.

SING > **Big, big, big and strong,**

The lions strut about.

Daniel doesn't worry, though,

'Cause God will work it out!

ask > **· Why are people afraid of lions?**

· Why didn't Daniel worry?

say > **The lion is a mighty animal! But it isn't stronger or mightier than God. Daniel didn't worry because he knew that God could take care of him. God will take care of us, too.**

PRAYERS

Care Prayer

Supplies: none

Have the children open up their arms as wide as they can, practicing what it would be like to give God a hug. Then have them fold their hands in their laps and "hold that hug" until the appropriate time in the prayer. Have the kids repeat each line after you.

 Dear God,

Thank you for hearing our worries, and

Thank you for caring for us.

If we could give you a hug,

It would look like this... (Have the children take turns stretching their arms wide as they say, "I love you more than this, God!")

Then have the children say together, "In Jesus' name, amen."

God Listens

Supplies: none

 Thank you, God, for listening when I pray.

I'll tell you my worries

Because I know that

You'll take care of me.

In Jesus' name, amen.

snacks

Den-tures

Supplies: bagels (cut in half), softened cream cheese or honey butter, pretzel sticks, raisins, plastic knives, plates, napkins

Have the kids wash their hands before they prepare the snacks. Have them make lions' heads by spreading cream cheese or honey butter on each bagel half and putting several pretzel sticks around each bagel to look like a mane. Then let the kids add raisins as eyes and noses. Tell the children each to make an X with two pretzel sticks where the lion's mouth would be to remind the children that God protected Daniel in the lions' den and closed the lions' mouths.

 Say ▶ **God took care of Daniel by closing the lions' mouths. God takes care of us, too, by giving us good friends and people who love us. Let's thank God for our snacks and for his care!**

Ask a child to pray, then let the kids open their mouths and eat the snacks!

A Mane Meal

Supplies: paper bowls, spoons, butterscotch pudding, vanilla wafers, decorator icing

Before beginning, spoon butterscotch pudding into paper bowls. Have kids wash their hands (or use wet wipes), then gather the children around a table.

Give each child a bowl of pudding and a vanilla wafer. Let children each place the wafer on top of the pudding to make a lion's face against a butterscotch mane. Provide decorator icing in tubes, and encourage children to draw eyes and mouths on their vanilla wafers. Choose a child to thank God for providing the snack and taking away worries. Then let kids enjoy eating their snack.

 ask ▶ • **How would you feel if you were close to a lion?**

• **What should you do when you're worried or afraid?**

• **How do you think Daniel felt when God closed the lions' mouths?**

say ▶ **God was stronger than the lions, and he closed the lions' mouths. God took care of Daniel. God takes care of us.**

"When I'm..." Rhyme

Supplies: none

Build excitement in your voice as you lead the children in saying and doing this rhyme together.

 When I'm praying by my bed, God is listening in. *(Lean over with one hand behind your ear.)*

When I'm singing in my room, God wears a great big grin. *(Draw a big smile on your face with your fingers.)*

When I'm laughing as I play, God can always see. *(Shade your eyes.)*

When I'm feeling scared or sad, God takes care of me. *(Hug yourself tightly.)*

GOD TELLS PEOPLE to Get Ready

Bible Basis:

> Isaiah 9:6; Jeremiah 33:14-16; Luke 3:7-18

Supplies:

Bible

Open your Bible to Luke 3, and show the children the words.

say Today's Bible story tells us we need to get ready for Jesus. Jesus' cousin, John the Baptist, was excited because Jesus was coming. He told everyone to get ready for Jesus.

When we're looking forward to someone coming, we get excited. We want to share the good news. In the Bible, John the Baptist left the desert where he'd been living and went into town. He was excited to tell everyone that Jesus was coming.

John wore clothes made of camel hair. Most likely his beard was long. The Bible says he ate honey and locusts.

John the Baptist went all over telling people to get ready for Jesus, the Savior God had promised. Let's act out the things John told people they needed to do to get ready for Jesus.

Use good actions toward other people, and do what's right. (Have kids hug each other.)

God's king is coming. (Have kids place both hands on top of their heads, and point them up with fingers touching to form a crown.)

Get ready now, tonight! (Have kids rub hands over their hearts.)

Forgive others! Share what you have. (Have children spread hands out in front slowly.)

Get ready for Jesus' coming. Praise God alone! (Have children point to heaven.)

"Are you the king?" the people asked. John said, "No, I'm not the king. But we must all get ready for Jesus. He is God's Son." John told people to get ready for Jesus. We need to get ready for Jesus, too.

ask • What's one thing John told the people to do?

• Do you think it would be hard to get ready as John said? Why?

• What's one good action you can show Jesus?

• What is one way you can get ready for Jesus?

Bible Experiences

God Was With Them

Supplies: Bible picture books

Place Bible picture books out for the children to look through to find times that God was with people. Have children form pairs, and have one partner slowly count to 10 while the other partner quickly looks for a situation showing that God was with someone. For example, a child might point to a picture of Daniel in the lions' den and say, "God was with Daniel when Daniel was in the lions' den."

ask
- **Who were some people God was with in the Bible? How did God help them?**
- **When was God with you or your family?**
- **How can we know that God keeps his promises?**

say **All through the Bible we can find examples where God was with people. God loves you and promises to be with you, too.**

Cleaning Up for Company

Supplies: magnifying glasses; large paper hearts cut from construction paper; tissues; different materials such as dirt, sand, salt, herbs

Set out magnifying glasses. Lay the hearts on the table, and sprinkle a different material such as dirt, sand, salt, or herbs onto each of the hearts.

Give kids the magnifying glasses, and let them walk from heart to heart examining the "dirt" and enlarging the objects that need cleaning up. Explain to the children that sometimes dirt is hidden and hard for us to find and clean up. When we say wrong things, it's like the dirt on our hearts—we can't see it, but it's there. Nobody can see it just by looking at us, but God sees our hearts. God wants our hearts to be clean, too.

ask
- **How do you feel when you've done something wrong?**
- **What are some things you can tell God you're sorry for?**
- **What does God do when we say we're sorry?**

Give kids tissues, and tell them to wipe the dirt off their hearts, and then look through their magnifying glasses again.

say **Sometimes it's not easy to see everything that needs cleaning. John the Baptist told people to clean up their lives and hearts for Jesus. We need to get ready for Jesus, too! John also wanted people to tell God they were sorry for any bad things they had done. John knew God would forgive them. When Jesus is your friend, all you have to do is ask, and he will forgive you and clean your heart, too!**

CRafts

"We Need Jesus" Puzzles

Supplies: old Christmas card fronts, resealable sandwich bags, scissors

Give each child the front of a Christmas card, a resealable sandwich bag, and a pair of scissors. Let the children cut the cards into five or six simple shapes to make a puzzle. When children have finished, ask them to exchange puzzles with a friend. Give them a few minutes to arrange all but one of the puzzle pieces.

say ▸ **Your puzzle needs one more piece in order to be complete. Without Jesus, our heart is like the puzzle that needs another piece.**

ask ▸ **• What do we need?**

• Why do you need Jesus?

say ▸ **We need Jesus. Jesus helps us when we're in trouble, he forgives us when we sin, and he shows us how to please God. God knew exactly what we needed, and that's why he sent his Son. Add the last piece to your puzzle, and thank God for giving you Jesus.**

Lead the children in prayer, and then have kids place their own puzzle pieces in the sandwich bags to take home.

Shining Hearts

Supplies: paper, crayons, plastic heart stencils

If you don't have plastic heart stencils, you can make stencils out of cardstock that the children can trace.

Distribute pieces of paper, and have children write their names on them. Set out the plastic heart stencils and crayons. Show the children how to hold the stencils down tightly on their papers with one hand and push the crayon from the edge of the stencils onto the paper to create heart designs. Tell the children to choose colors that show how they feel after God has forgiven them.

Encourage them to create many shining hearts of different colors all over their papers.

ask ▸ **• What are some things that kids do that they need to ask forgiveness for?**

• How do you feel after someone forgives you?

• What do we need to do to get ready for Jesus?

say ▸ **We all do mean things sometimes and need Jesus to forgive us. We need to get ready for Jesus by saying we're sorry when we do something wrong and asking him to forgive us.**

Wipe Your Heart Clean

Supplies: white paper, wax paper cut into a heart shape for each child, glue, washable markers, wet wipes

Distribute the paper and have kids write their names on them. Give each child a wax-paper heart, and encourage the kids to glue the wax paper so that it covers their pages. Remind the children that sin makes our hearts dirty. We get our hearts ready for Jesus by asking for forgiveness. Encourage kids to each draw a picture of a sin (such as not sharing toys) that they want Jesus to help clean up. Have children say this together: "We need to get ready for Jesus." Then have the kids use the wet wipes to remove the "sins" from the hearts on their pages.

ask
- **What sins did you draw?**
- **Why do we need Jesus?**
- **Who can you tell about Jesus' love and forgiveness?**

say When we say we're sorry, Jesus forgives us and cleans our hearts. Let's tell everyone how much Jesus loves them and forgives them. Let's help everyone get ready for Jesus.

Games

Ready, Set, Go!

Supplies: hearts made out of paper and crumpled, fresh flat hearts, large paper cross, tape

Tape the cross to the wall. Set the "clean" hearts on the floor below the cross.

 We've learned that John was helping people get ready for Jesus to come. He told the people to get their hearts ready. John told them to be sorry for their sin and ask God's forgiveness. He was saying, "Get ready. Get set. Jesus is coming soon!"

Have the children line up in two rows for a relay race. Give each of them a crumpled heart.

 The people needed God to take away their sin and make their hearts clean and new. That's why Jesus was coming. Jesus would one day take all of sin's punishment and die for it on the cross. John was helping others get ready to believe in Jesus and to take their sin to the cross where it could be forgiven. Let's take our yucky sinful hearts and run to the cross. When you get there, lay down your crumpled heart and come back with a clean, new heart. Get ready. Get set. Go!

After everyone has exchanged their hearts, ask them to sit down in a circle.

 • Where did you go to get your clean heart?

• What did John want the people to do?

• What does God want you to do?

 John told people to ask God's forgiveness and to make their hearts clean and new. We need to get ready for Jesus by making our hearts new and clean, too.

- -

Clean Hands, Clean Hearts

Supplies: plastic tablecloth, two dishpans, water, bar of soap, several towels

At one side of the room, lay out a plastic tablecloth. On top of it, place two dishpans of water, a bar of soap, and several towels.

Ask the kids to line up on one side of the room for a relay. When you say "go," the children will one at a time run to the first dishpan, dip their hands into the water, use the soap, rinse their hands in the second pan of water, dry their hands, and run back to the line. As the runner tags the next child in line, he or she will say, "We need to get ready for Jesus."

ask · What makes us dirty?

· How do we become clean?

· What makes our hearts dirty?

· How does Jesus clean us from our sins?

say We use soap and water to clean up from dirt and germs. We get ready for Jesus and welcome him into our lives when we say we're sorry. Jesus cleans us from our sins!

John in the Desert

Supplies: 2 dishpans, sand, scoop or spoon, clothespins, markers

Remind children that John the Baptist told others to stop doing bad things and start doing what was right. He wanted people to get ready for Jesus! Have the kids take turns scooping sand from one dishpan into the other. For each scoop of sand, have the children say a sin, such as fighting or name-calling. Then have the kids each draw a face on a clothespin and take turns pretending to be John the Baptist in the sandy desert. Kids can tell others to say that they're sorry for their sins and to get ready for Jesus.

ask · What did John the Baptist tell people?

· What sins, or things you've done wrong, are you sorry for?

· How can Jesus clean your heart from those wrong things?

say John told everyone to get ready for Jesus and to stop doing bad things! Sometimes it's hard to share our toys or to remember to speak kindly. But Jesus can help us. When we sin, we can ask for forgiveness. We can listen to Bible stories and learn how Jesus wants us to act.

Tell kids to take home their John the Baptist clothespins to use to tell others today's story.

PRAYERS

"Help Me" Prayer

Supplies: cross

Have the children kneel at the foot of the cross as they repeat this prayer after you.

 Help me, Lord, at home and play
To remember to obey.
Clean my heart and help me know
That you love me as I grow.
In Jesus' name, amen.

"Clean My Heart" Prayer

Supplies: none

Have children sit in a circle on the floor. Tell kids to think of one thing they've done wrong, and then tell them to repeat this prayer after you:

 **Dear God,**
Make our hearts clean; help us get ready today.
Prepare our hearts for Jesus, so he can come to stay.
In Jesus' name, amen.

People Get Ready

Supplies: none

Let the children pretend they're John, telling people to get ready for Jesus. Starting with the child on your right as "John," have him or her tell another child to get ready for Jesus. Encourage the second child to respond with the following prayer.

 Dear God, help me to get ready for Jesus.
In Jesus' name we pray, amen.

Go around the circle, letting each child participate, until all have had a turn to be John and to pray.

snacks

A Popcorn Surprise

Supplies: microwave popcorn, cups

Have children wash their hands before beginning this activity.

say ▶ **Let's thank God for being with us and for providing our snack.** Invite one child to pray for the snack. Then hold up a package of microwavable popcorn so the children can see the words written on the package.

ask ▶ • **What do you think the words on this package are promising us?**

• **Do you think the promise will come true? Why or why not?**

say ▶ **The people who made this package promise us that the kernels inside will turn into popcorn if we put this package in the microwave for** [package timing directions] **minutes. Let's follow the directions, and see if they keep their promise to us.** Place the package in the microwave, and allow kids to watch and listen. **Just as the package promised, these tiny kernels turned into big, fluffy pieces of popcorn.**

ask ▶ • **How is this package like God's promises to us? How is it different?**

say ▶ **This package promises us popcorn. We can trust that it won't pop peanut butter or ice cream. God promised to send Jesus, and he did. God always keeps his promises.**

After the popcorn finishes popping, have the children sit down. Fill small cups with the popped corn, and let kids enjoy the snack.

- -

"Clean Heart" Snacks

Supplies: heart-shaped cookie cutters, clear gelatin (made with the "Jigglers" recipe in a shallow pan), cups, water or white grape juice

Let children use heart-shaped cookie cutters to cut heart shapes in the clear gelatin. Give kids cups of water or white grape juice to drink with their heart snacks.

ask ▶ • **How does it feel knowing that Jesus wants to make you clean on the inside?**

• **How did John tell the people to prepare for Jesus?**

• **What are some ways we can prepare our hearts for Jesus?**

say ▶ **The people who heard John speak knew that they needed to get ready for Jesus. John gave them many examples to help them be kind to others. John also told them that only Jesus could make their hearts really clean. We need to get ready for Jesus, too!**

God Keeps His Promises

Supplies: none

Have children join you in singing "God Keeps His Promises" to the tune of the chorus of "Oh, How I Love Jesus."

SING God has kept his promises.
God has kept his promises.
God has kept his promises.
He'll take all my sins away.

Jesus came to save us.
Jesus came to save us.
Jesus came to save us
And take all my sins away.

We Know God Is With Us

Supplies: none

Sing "We Know God Is With Us" to the tune of "He's Got the Whole World in His Hands." Encourage the children to join you in singing.

SING We know God is with us, yes he is.
We know God is with us, yes he is.
We know God is with us, yes he is.
We know he promised to be here.

Jesus Is Born

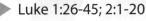

Bible Basis:

> Luke 1:26-45; 2:1-20

Supplies:

Bible, doll, blanket, box or cradle

Open your Bible to Luke 1, and show the children the words.

say **Today's Bible story tells us that Jesus was born.**

Select four kids to repeat after you the words of Gabriel, Mary, Elizabeth, and the Angel. Let the other children in your class act out the parts of baby John, the shepherds, the sheep, and Mary and Joseph at the manger. Wrap a doll in a blanket to represent baby Jesus, and place the doll in a box or cradle. Read the dialogue below, pausing to let the child playing each part repeat the words after you.

Gabriel: Hi, Mary! I'm the angel Gabriel. (Have child repeat.) Don't be afraid! (Have child repeat.) God has chosen you to give birth to his Son. (Have child repeat.) You are to name the child Jesus. (Have child repeat.)

Mary: Is this true? (Have child repeat.) What will I do? (Have child repeat.)

Gabriel: Don't worry. (Have child repeat.) God will take care of you and the baby. (Have child repeat.) Your cousin Elizabeth is going to have a baby, too! (Have child repeat.) Her baby will grow up to tell everyone about Jesus. (Have child repeat.)

Mary: I will do whatever God wants! (Have child repeat.)

Narrator (Teacher): Then Mary went to visit Elizabeth. When Mary said hello to Elizabeth, baby John inside Elizabeth's tummy jumped for joy!

Children: (Have children jump up and down.)

Elizabeth: (with an excited and loud voice) God has blessed you and your baby! (Have child repeat.) You are the mother of the Son of God! (Have child repeat.) The baby in my tummy jumped when he heard your voice! (Have child repeat.)

Children: (Have children jump up and down.)

Narrator (Teacher): Mary stayed with Elizabeth for a while before going back home. Later, on the night that Jesus was born, angels appeared to shepherds who were out in the fields watching their flocks.

Children: (Have some children stand up and pretend to watch the sheep while other kids pretend to be sheep.)

Angel: Don't be afraid. (Have child repeat.) I bring good news! (Have child repeat.) Jesus is born! (Have child repeat.) Follow the bright star to where he is. (Have child repeat.) You'll find Jesus sleeping in a manger. (Have child repeat.)

Narrator (Teacher): The shepherds were so excited because they had been waiting a long time for Jesus to be born—Jesus was here at last! So the shepherds went to Bethlehem to see Jesus and worship him.

Children: (Have children walk over to the doll representing baby Jesus, then have kids sit down. Choose two children to sit by baby Jesus and pretend to be Mary and Joseph.)

Narrator (Teacher): The shepherds found baby Jesus lying in a manger just like the angel had told them. Angels sang, and the shepherds worshipped Jesus, the Son of God. All of heaven was happy that Jesus was born!

Children: (Shout together) Jesus is born! Jesus is born!

BiBLe eXPeRienCes

Announcing!

Supplies: dolls, baby supplies, toy telephones, microphones, chalk and a chalkboard, paper, pencils

Set out dolls and baby supplies, toy telephones, microphones, chalk and a chalkboard, paper and pencils. Encourage children to think of as many ways as possible to tell others about the birth of Jesus. Have them take turns using the supplies to share the good news with others in the class.

ask • **What's your favorite way to tell others about Jesus?**

• **This week, how will you tell someone about Jesus' birth?**

say **There are lots of ways to tell the good news of Jesus' birth. See if you can use one of the ways we talked about today to tell someone that Jesus was born!**

Babies, Babies, Babies

Supplies: broad range of baby pictures from birth to 12 months (pictures can be from your family or from books or magazines)

Have kids look at the pictures of babies and find the pictures they like the best. Encourage children to discover the baby with the most hair or the biggest eyes.

> **ask** • Why do you like the picture you chose?
>
> • Would you like to have a baby like this living at your house? Why or why not?
>
> • What do you think Jesus looked like when he was a baby? acted like? sounded like?

> **say** I'm sure that before Jesus was born, Mary wondered what her baby would look like—most moms and dads wonder about their babies. The Bible doesn't tell us what Jesus looked like, but we do know that Jesus was born, and he grew up just like we grow up.

Make Room for Jesus

Supplies: a variety of shapes and sizes of blocks

Set out the blocks. Remind kids that Jesus is God and that he came to earth to live with us. Ask children to pretend that Jesus is coming to visit. What would they put in a room where Jesus would be staying? Have the children arrange the blocks according to their ideas.

> **ask** • What did you put in your special room for Jesus?
>
> • How do you feel knowing that Jesus wants you to live with him forever?
>
> • How can you thank Jesus for coming to help you?

> **say** Jesus is God! Jesus loves us so much that he wants us to live forever with him in heaven.

CRafts

Bells of Praise

Supplies: red chenille wire, white chenille wire, small jingle bells, photocopies of song lyrics

Give each child one red and one white chenille wire and two small jingle bells. Help children twist the two chenille wires together so they look like candy canes. Leave about 2 inches from the top of each wire untwisted. Slide a jingle bell on the end of each wire. Secure the bell by folding the end of the wire over and then twisting it back. Encourage kids to shake their bells as they sing this song to the tune of "London Bridge."

SING ▷ **Jesus Christ was born today,**

Born today, born today!

Jesus Christ was born today!

Let's celebrate!

Make a copy of the song for each child to take home as a reminder of today's story.

PRayeRs

Jesus' Light Prayer

Supplies: string of Christmas lights, flashlight, picture of Jesus

Have the children sit on the floor in two rows facing each other, with the string of lights between them. Plug in the lights. You'll also need the flashlight with Jesus' picture attached to it.

One at a time, have each child hold the flashlight. Affirm each child by saying, "I can see Jesus' light in [child's name]," then add a statement such as "when she shares toys with her friend," "when he helps clean up our room," or "when she tells others about Jesus."

As a prayer, let each child say, "Jesus is God and lives in me." At the end, have everyone close the prayer by saying with you, "In Jesus' name, amen."

Great News Prayer

Supplies: none

Ask children to think of good news they could share about Jesus. For example, kids might say, "Jesus loves me," "Jesus saves us," "We'll live forever because of Jesus," or "Jesus is God." Go around the circle and have each child tell the good news. After each child shares, have everyone pray, "Thank you, God, that Jesus was born." After everyone has shared, ask all of the children to join you in ending the prayer by saying, "In Jesus' name, amen."

"Jesus Is Born" Prayer

Supplies: baby doll wrapped in a blanket

Have the children sit in a circle with their legs crossed. Wrap a baby doll in a blanket, and pass the doll around the circle. Instruct the children to say the following prayer as they hold the doll.

PRAY **Dear God,**
Thank you for sending Jesus
To be born for us.
In Jesus' name, amen.

snacks

Jesus Is God

Supplies: can of frosting, gingerbread cookies (two per child), napkins, plastic knives

Tell the children to wash their hands, then have the kids make snacks to remind them that Jesus is God. Let each child use a plastic knife to spread frosting on a cookie and top the cookie with another cookie. Have the children each look at the top cookie and say, "Jesus is God." Then have the kids turn over their cookie sandwiches and say, "God is Jesus. They are one!" Invite a child to pray, then let the kids eat and enjoy the snacks.

ask
- **Why did Jesus come from heaven?**
- **How can you thank Jesus for coming from heaven?**

say Jesus is God, and God is Jesus. They are one! Jesus wants us to live with him in heaven forever. Let's tell everyone about Jesus.

Edible News

Supplies: sliced bread, frosting in a decorator bag (or in a resealable plastic bag with a very small hole in one corner)

Have children wash their hands. Then give each child a slice of bread and the bag of frosting you prepared before class. Show children how to squeeze the frosting through the corner of the bag so they can "write" on the slice of bread. (Lines and squiggles are fine!) Tell kids to pretend they are writing a newspaper story about Jesus' birth. Encourage children to share their stories with each other.

Pray and thank God for sending his Son, Jesus, then encourage kids to eat their "newspapers."

ask
- **How can you spread the good news that Jesus is born?**
- **What can you tell people about Jesus?**

say We can share the good news that Jesus was born with everyone we know!

"Rock-a-Bye Jesus" Snacks

Supplies: alfalfa sprouts, baby carrots, sliced celery, paper plates

Place alfalfa sprouts, baby carrots, and the celery on plates, and set the plates on a table for the children to serve themselves and prepare their snacks.

Before beginning, have the children wash their hands or use wet wipes or disinfectant hand gel. Have children sit at the table, and invite one child to pray for the snacks.

Give kids each a small plate. Let kids create a manger scene using the celery as the manger, sprouts to represent straw, and carrots to represent baby Jesus. Encourage kids to rock baby Jesus to sleep as they sing the song, and remind kids that Jesus was born for us.

SING **Silent night! Holy night!**
All is calm, all is bright
'Round yon virgin mother and child.
Holy infant, so tender and mild,
Sleep in heavenly peace,
Sleep in heavenly peace.

Mary Heard the Angel

Supplies: baby doll wrapped in a blanket

Have the children stand in a circle. Choose a child to be the angel Gabriel and hold a doll to represent baby Jesus. As the class sings "Mary Heard the Angel" to the tune of "The Mulberry Bush," have "Gabriel" walk around the inside of the circle getting ready to choose a Mary. At the end of the song, have Gabriel hand "baby Jesus" to the "Mary" of his or her choice. The child chosen then becomes the angel Gabriel, and the game continues. Continue to play, allowing as many children to have a turn as time allows.

SING
> **Mary heard the angel say,**
> **Angel say, angel say.**
> **Mary heard the angel say**
> **That Jesus would be born.**
> **Jesus is God's only Son,**
> **God's only Son, God's only Son.**
> **Jesus is God's only Son.**
> **His mother was Mary.**

JESUS GROWS UP

Bible Basis:

Luke 2:39-52

Supplies:

Bible

Open your Bible to Luke 2, and show the children the words.

say Today's Bible story tells us that Jesus is special. Let's find out what happened when Jesus was a boy.

I need everyone to listen closely to the Bible story. When you hear the name "Jesus," I want you to make the sign for Jesus by touching your middle finger to the palm of the opposite hand and then your other middle finger to the palm of your other hand. Pause for practice. **When you hear the name "Mary," open your mouth wide and hold your hands up to your mouth like this.** Show the gesture, and have kids repeat it.

ask • Have you ever gone to a party or a celebration with lots of family and friends together?

say The Bible tells us about a time Jesus' (show sign for Jesus) **family had a big party. Let's listen carefully for the words "Mary"** (show sign for Mary) **and "Jesus"** (show sign for Jesus). **Great! Let's begin.**

When Jesus (show sign) was 12 years old, he went with Mary (show sign) and Joseph to Jerusalem. Lots of his aunts, uncles, and cousins went, too. So did their neighbors. They went there to celebrate a special holiday, and Jerusalem was full of people.

When it was time to go home, Mary (show sign) and Joseph couldn't find Jesus (show sign). They decided he must have gone on ahead with one of his relatives. It wasn't until the next day they realized Jesus (show sign) was not with anyone in the family. Mary (show sign) and Joseph turned around and walked back to Jerusalem to find Jesus (show sign). The town was still very crowded, and they couldn't see Jesus (show sign) anywhere.

Mary (show sign) and Joseph asked everyone they saw, "Have you seen Jesus (show sign)?" The people shook their heads sadly and said, "No, we're sorry, we haven't."

Mary (show sign) **and Joseph searched for Jesus** (show sign) **for three whole days, but they couldn't find him. Finally, Mary** (show sign) **and Joseph looked in the Temple. In the Temple they saw a group of priests and teachers. All of them were listening to a young boy.**

ask ▸ · **Who do you think that young boy was?**

say ▸ **The boy was Jesus** (show sign)**!**

Mary (show sign) **and Joseph were excited, but upset, too. They walked up to Jesus** (show sign)**. "Why didn't you come back with us?" they asked. "We were so worried."**

Jesus (show sign) **seemed surprised. "Didn't you know I'd be in my Father's house?" Mary** (show sign) **understood that when Jesus** (show sign) **said, "my Father," he meant God, his heavenly Father. She understood that her son was very special, that he and the Father were one.**

ask ▸ · **How did Mary and Joseph feel when they thought Jesus was lost?**

· **Were they surprised when they found Jesus? Why or why not?**

· **How do you think they felt when they knew Jesus was in the house of his heavenly Father?**

say ▸ **Mary and Joseph were so happy to find Jesus. They knew Jesus was God's special Son.**

CRafts

Jesus in the Temple

Supplies: paper, crayons or markers

Fold each piece of paper in on both sides so that the folded parts look like doors. Help the children draw pictures of Joseph and Mary on the outside of the Temple, looking for Jesus. Then have children draw a picture of Jesus and the teachers on the inside of the Temple. When the children open the doors, they'll find Jesus in the Temple, just as Joseph and Mary did.

ask ▸ · **How did Mary and Joseph feel when they thought Jesus was lost?**

· **What was unusual about what Jesus was doing when Mary and Joseph found him?**

say ▸ **Mary and Joseph learned that Jesus was very special when they found him in the Temple.**

Games

Where Is Jesus?

Supplies: small doll or action figure

Give kids the small doll or action figure to represent Jesus. Have the children sit in a circle and hide their eyes. Choose one child to hide "Jesus." After the child has hidden the toy, have him or her come back and sit with the other children. Have kids open their eyes. As the children search for "Jesus," as Mary and Joseph did, have kids chant the following poem. When "Jesus" is found, have all the kids return to the circle and begin the game again, choosing another child to hide "Jesus."

say ▶ **Jesus is special,**

Born of God,

Sent from heaven

To show us God's love.

After everyone has had a chance to hide the toy, ask the children the following questions.

ask ▶ **• How do you think Mary and Joseph felt when they were looking for Jesus?**

• Have you ever looked for something for a long time? How did you feel when you finally found it?

say ▶ **Mary and Joseph searched everywhere until they finally found their special son. Aren't you glad Jesus is special?**

Looking for Jesus

Supplies: none

Have kids take turns pretending to be Jesus, his parents, and the priests in acting out the story. "Parents" could call out "Jesus, where are you?" a few times. Encourage the children to look for the missing boy. Then have "Jesus" pop out and say, "Here I am." Continue until several have had a chance to play "Jesus."

ask ▶ **• Have your parents ever thought you were lost when you knew just where they were? What happened?**

• What should you do if you're lost?

say ▶ **In our story, Jesus was safe in his heavenly Father's house. God knew where he was and provided people to take care of Jesus, because Jesus is special.**

"Finding Jesus" Card Game

Supplies: index cards (6 per child), crayons, envelopes (1 per child)

Have the children sit together around tables. Give each child six index cards and crayons, and instruct children to draw a picture of Jesus on one of the cards.

> **say** One of our cards is special. It's different from all the others. Jesus is special, too. He's the Savior that God sent to the world. No one else can take away our sin, and those who believe in Jesus can become children of God.

Let each child shuffle his or her cards together so that the Jesus card is mixed in with the rest. Children may play in pairs or trios. Have children spread out one set of cards, facedown, on the table in front of the team.

> **say** Jesus is special to God, but he was also special to Mary and Joseph. When they could not find him in the big city of Jerusalem, they were very worried. They searched and searched until they finally found him.

Each child will take a turn looking for Jesus by flipping over one card at a time until the Jesus card is found. The child who finds Jesus should shout, "Jesus is special."

> **ask** • How did it feel to find Jesus?
>
> • Why was Jesus special to Mary and Joseph?
>
> • Why is Jesus special to you?

Let each child place his or her cards in an envelope to take home and play with others.

PRaYeRS

Growing-Up Prayer

Supplies: none

Have the children begin this fun prayer by standing with their hands at their sides. Then have kids do the motions as they repeat the lines.

> **PRay** Dear Jesus,
>
> You were once small like me. *(Squat down.)*
>
> You know what I want to be. *(Point up.)*
>
> Help me to grow strong and true *(stand up slowly)*
>
> As I keep on loving you. *(Hug yourself.)*
>
> In Jesus' name, amen.

snacks

Wide-Eyed Snack

Supplies: paper plates, plastic knives, round crackers, frosting, banana slices, raisins

> **say** For three days Mary and Joseph looked for Jesus in the big city of Jerusalem. They opened their eyes wide as they searched all through Jerusalem. Jesus was special to Mary and Joseph, and Jesus is special to us, too. Let's make a snack that has wide eyes as we talk about how special Jesus is to us.

Let the children create "eyes" by spreading the frosting on the crackers and placing a banana slice and raisin in the middle of each one.

> **say** Mary and Joseph found Jesus in the Temple. He was having a wonderful time talking about God with all of the teachers there. Mary and Joseph loved Jesus as their son, but they also loved him as God's Son. They knew that he was a very special boy who would grow up to be the one who would forgive sin.

> **ask** • Why is Jesus special to you?
>
> • What other words tell what Jesus is like?

Special Snacks

Supplies: plain wafer cookies, paper plates, frosting, plastic knives, sprinkles

Give each child a few plain wafer cookies on a paper plate and a plastic knife, and set the remaining materials nearby. Encourage your children to create very special cookies using the frosting and the sprinkles.

> **say** Jesus was not like everyone else. Jesus is special. You started with cookies that were just like everyone else's cookies, but now you have very special cookies. Before we eat our cookies, let's remember to thank God for sending his special Son, Jesus, to us.

Invite one child to pray for the snack.

God's Special Son

Supplies: none

Sing "Do You Know God's Special Son?" to the tune of "The Muffin Man."

SING
Do you know God's special Son? *(Point to a friend.)*
He and God are really one. *(Bring palms together.)*
Do you know God's special Son? *(Point to a friend.)*
It's Jesus Christ the Lord. *(Point up to heaven.)*

Yes, I know God's special Son. *(Point to self.)*
He and God are really one. *(Bring palms together.)*
Yes, I know God's special Son. *(Point to self.)*
It's Jesus Christ the Lord. *(Point to heaven.)*

ASK
• **Who is God's special Son?**

• **What can happen if you believe in Jesus?**

SAY
Jesus is special, and if you believe in him, you can become a child of God.

Jesus Calls the Disciples

Bible Basis:

Mark 1:16-20

Supplies:

Bible, brown bedsheet or blanket, masking tape, towel or small lace tablecloth

Before class, use the brown sheet to create a shoreline, and create an outline of a boat on the floor using masking tape.

Have the children gather near the "shoreline" and "boat." Choose children to pretend to be James, John, and Zebedee, and have them sit in the masking tape boat and pretend to fish. Choose other children to play the parts of Jesus, Simon, and Andrew. Have the child playing Jesus walk along the shoreline, and have the children playing Simon and Andrew stand and pretend to fish from the shore, using a towel or small lace tablecloth as a "fishing net." Have the rest of the children pretend to be fishermen, either fishing from the boat or fishing and mending nets on the shore.

Open your Bible to Mark 1, and show children the words.

say **Today's Bible story teaches us that we need to follow Jesus.**

Jesus went to a town in Galilee and taught people about God. As he taught, he looked for people who were listening very carefully. Jesus wanted special friends who were very good listeners. Jesus wanted people who loved to listen to God's Word.

Have the child acting as Jesus stand a short distance from "Simon" and "Andrew."

say **As Jesus walked along the shores of the Sea of Galilee, he saw two brothers holding a fishing net. Their names were Simon and Andrew, and they were fishermen.** Have "Jesus" stop to talk to Simon and Andrew.

ask • **What do you think Jesus said to Simon and Andrew?**

say **Jesus said, "Come, follow me, and I will show you how to fish for people!" So the two brothers dropped their net, and they followed Jesus.** Have the two children drop their net, line up behind Jesus, and follow him. **As Jesus continued along the shore, he saw two more brothers who were fishermen. They were with their father in his boat. The brothers' names were James and John. Jesus waved to the brothers.** Have the child pretending to be Jesus wave. **And the two brothers waved back.** Have "James" and "John" wave.

Jesus said, "Come, follow me, and I will show you how to fish for people!" And they did. They left their nets and waved goodbye to their father and the other fishermen. Have the children pretending to be James and John walk away from the boat outline and wave goodbye. **Their father and the fishermen waved goodbye to James and John.** Have "Zebedee" wave to James and John. Have James and John join the line behind the child pretending to be Jesus.

ask ▶ • **Why do you think the disciples wanted to follow Jesus?**

• **What would you say to Jesus?**

say ▶ **James, John, Simon, and Andrew became Jesus' special friends. Jesus chose his special friends to help him do his work on earth. Jesus called the fishermen to come follow him, and he is still calling us today to come follow him!**

BiBLe eXPeRienCes

Parade of Followers

Supplies: CD player, CD with some sort of "parade" music

Prompt children to start an animal parade! (You'll need to help the first child with this, then once other kids join in you can step out and watch.)

Explain that kids should pick an animal they'd like to be and then act like the animal as they follow each other around the room in a line. They should "walk" like the animal (or waddle, or crawl, or whatever is applicable) and make animal noises. Play appropriate parade music, such as "The Stars and Stripes Forever" or another great marching song. (If you'd rather, you can give kids parade supplies such as drums, pompoms, and other noisemakers.) Cheer them on as they follow each other around the room!

Wrap up the parade by telling kids that today they learned about following Jesus, just like they followed the leader of the parade.

CRAFTS

Noodle Walk

Supplies: cooked and cooled (still soft) noodles (10-inch pieces of string will also work), paper with a path drawn on it (draw an original, and photocopy one for each kid), paint, smocks

Distribute the paper and have the kids write their names on them. Have children put on paint smocks. Then they can dip the noodles into the paint and drag the noodles along the "path that Jesus walked to town." Encourage kids to continue to dip the noodles into paint and "draw" as needed to complete the path.

ask • Was it hard or easy to follow Jesus' path on the page? Why?

• How can we follow Jesus today?

• How can we help our friends follow Jesus?

say Following Jesus can be fun and exciting! Jesus did so many wonderful things. When we follow Jesus, we can do some of the wonderful things he did, like caring for people and teaching others about God.

Footprints

Supplies: paper, markers, Jesus pictures (1 per child), glue, washable ink pads, wet wipes

Give each child a piece of paper and a marker. Encourage children to each draw a path on their paper and then glue a Jesus picture to the end of the path. Set out ink pads that children can share. Show kids how to press their first two fingers into the ink and then press them onto the paper path to make "footprints." Encourage kids to shout out some ways they can follow Jesus as they "walk" their fingers and make footprints along the paths to Jesus.

ask • How do you think the disciples felt following Jesus?

• Would you like to follow Jesus? Why or why not?

say It was probably hard sometimes for the disciples to follow Jesus, but they knew it was worth it. We can believe in Jesus and follow him, too. We know that if we believe in Jesus and follow him, we will live forever with him in heaven.

Games

Jesus Came to Town

Supplies: none

say ▸ **Let's play a game and pretend we're following Jesus.**

Help the children play a game similar to "The Farmer in the Dell" as they sing a song to the same tune. Have the children form a circle, and choose one child to play the part of Jesus. Have the child playing Jesus walk around the inside of the circle as you lead the children in singing the first four lines. At line five, have "Jesus" choose a child to follow him. At the end of the eighth line, the two children will be standing in the center of the circle.

Repeat the third verse with the last child chosen becoming the "chooser," until every child has been chosen and is standing in the center of the no-longer-existent circle. Sing the fourth verse to end the game.

sing ▸ **Jesus came to town.**
He shared the love of God.
Hallelujah! God is here!
Come follow him today.

He shared God's love with [chosen child's name]**.**
He shared God's love with [chosen child's name]**.**
Hallelujah! God is here!
Come follow him today.

[Chooser's name] **tells** [chosen child's name]**.**
[Chooser's name] **tells** [second child's name]**.**
Hallelujah! God is here!
Come follow him today.

No one stands alone.
No one stands alone.
Hallelujah! God is here!
Come follow him today.

ask ▸ • **How did you feel when you were chosen to follow "Jesus"?**

• **How do you think the disciples felt when Jesus picked them?**

• **What are some ways we can tell others about Jesus?**

say ▸ **Jesus loves us, and Jesus wants everyone in the world to follow him. We can help others follow Jesus by telling them that Jesus loves them and wants to know them better.**

PRAYERS

"I Want to Follow You"

Supplies: none

Have the children form a circle and do the actions as you say the prayer.

PRAY **Thank you, God, for calling me** (fold hands in prayer)
To come and follow you. (Walk in place.)
As I sit here with my friends today (take hands),
Lord, I want to follow you. (Nod head.)
I'll listen and obey your words (put hand behind ear to listen);
I know you'll help me, too. (Fold hands in prayer.)
In Jesus' name, amen.

snacks

Fishers of Men

Supplies: bedsheet, gummy bears, clothespins, strings

Hang up a bedsheet by attaching string to two opposite points, draping the sheet over the string, and securing it with clothespins. Have children wash their hands before this activity.

say **When the disciples dropped their nets and left their boats to follow Jesus, they became fishers of men. We say this because instead of catching fish in their nets, they were gathering people to believe in God. Now we'll pretend that these gummy bears are people. Let's go fishing for men!**

The children can take turns casting the line over the sheet while another child attaches a gummy bear to the clothespin. Children can reel in their catch for a yummy snack.

ask **• What did you like about our fishing game?**

• Have you ever told someone about Jesus? What happened?

• How can you help others follow Jesus?

say **Jesus told the disciples, "Come, follow me." Jesus told others about God's love, and he wants us to tell others, too!**

Sailing Snacks

Supplies: blue paper plates, fish crackers, toothpicks, hardboiled eggs (half per child), white paper triangles, tape

Give each child a blue paper plate, several fish-shaped crackers, a toothpick, half of a hard-boiled egg, and one of the white paper triangles you cut out before class.

Help children make "sails" by taping a white paper triangle to the top of a toothpick. Encourage each child to push the sail into the middle of the hard-boiled egg and then put the "boat" on the blue paper plate. Suggest that children pretend their plates are the water where the boats sail and the fish crackers swim.

ask
- **How do you think the men felt when Jesus told them to follow him?**
- **How can you choose to follow Jesus in your own life?**
- **How can you "fish for men" as Jesus asked the disciples to do?**

say **The disciples were excited and happy to follow Jesus. They knew that Jesus was special, and they wanted to help him. We can all choose to follow Jesus by believing in Jesus and doing the things Jesus did. Let's tell the world about Jesus so everyone will want to follow Jesus!**

SONGS

"Follow Jesus" Rhyme

Supplies: towel

The following rhyme can be said or it can be sung to the tune of "If You're Happy and You Know It." Have the children act it out. Have one child pretend to be Jesus and four others pretend to be Simon, Andrew, James, and John. The child pretending to be Jesus should stand at the front of the class; the children pretending to be the two sets of brothers should stand some distance away, slightly separated. Have "Simon" and "Andrew" hold a towel between them. At the lines "So they followed, followed Jesus all the way," the four "fishermen" should follow "Jesus" around the room. Then have the actors each choose a child to take his or her place. Continue the game until everyone has had a turn. Remind children that they can follow Jesus.

 Jesus said while on the shores of Galilee *(Jesus beckons disciples to follow him for first two lines)*,

"If you hear my voice now, follow me."

So Simon dropped his net while Andrew got all set *(Simon and Andrew drop towel)*,

And they grabbed James and John, sons of Zebedee. *(Simon and Andrew take the hands of James and John and go to Jesus.)*

So they followed, followed Jesus all the way. *(Jesus leads disciples around the room for last four lines.)*

So they followed, followed Jesus all the way.

From their boats to the streets, they told people every day,

To follow, follow Jesus all the way.

Jesus Turns Water Into Wine

Bible Basis:

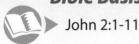 John 2:1-11

Supplies:

Bible, paper cups, blue and red drinks (such as Kool-Aid) in pitchers

Hand each child an empty paper cup. Open your Bible to John 2, and show the children the words.

say **Today's Bible story tells us that Jesus can do miracles. In our Bible story today, Jesus and his disciples go to a wedding.**

ask **• Have you ever seen a wedding? What do you know about weddings?**

say **There must have been many people at this wedding. Before long, all the drinks were gone, and there wasn't anything for the guests to drink! All of their cups were empty, and the wedding guests were thirsty!** Have the children hold their empty cups upside down. **Jesus and his mother, Mary, were at the wedding. When she heard there wasn't anything left to drink, she told Jesus, and Jesus told the servants to fill six large jars with water.** Have children turn their cups upright, and pour a very small amount of blue drink into the children's cups.

Jesus told the servants to fill the jars to the top. Pour some of the red drink into the children's cups, and let kids watch what happens.

Oh, look what happened! First the drink was blue, now it's purple. When I mixed blue and red together, they made purple. That's how I changed the color of the drinks. But do you know what Jesus did to the water at the wedding? Jesus changed the water into wine.

Make a very surprised face. **say** **Look at my face. Now show me what I look like.** Let children show you their surprised faces.

The disciples were so surprised! They knew Jesus was the Son of God, because only Jesus can do miracles!

Let the children enjoy their drinks as you ask questions about today's story.

ask **• How would you feel if you saw Jesus do a miracle today?**

• Why do you think Jesus turned the water into wine?

> **say** ▷ **I knew the color of the drink would change because I knew that blue and red together make purple. But only Jesus can do miracles, like changing water into wine or healing a person who is sick. Jesus can do these miracles because he is the Son of God.**

Bible Experiences

The Miracle of Growth

Supplies: paper cups, potting soil, flower seeds, water

Hand out the cups to the children. Help children fill their cups about three-fourths full with the potting soil. Show kids how to make a hole for their seeds by pushing a finger about an inch down into the soil. Let them each drop three to five seeds into the hole, then push the soil to cover the seeds. Then let kids moisten the soil with water, and place their cups in the classroom window.

> **ask** ▷ • **When we return next week, what miracle do you think we'll see?**

> **say** ▷ **We'll see a miracle! Jesus can do miracles.**

Crafts

Color Change Surprise

Supplies: pictures of a drinking glass (draw one, and make copies for all the kids), small cups of pink-lemonade drink mix, glue, markers or crayons

Distribute the papers. Set out several small cups of pink-lemonade powdered drink mix. Give kids markers or crayons, and have kids write their names on their papers. Give kids white glue, and tell them to use their fingers to spread a thin layer of glue in the drinking glass on their papers. Then show the children how to lightly sprinkle some of the drink mix over the glue. As the drink mix touches the moisture of the glue, a color change surprise will take place!

> **ask** ▷ • **What happened when you sprinkled the powdered drink mix on your papers?**
>
> • **How was the surprising color change like the miracle Jesus performed when he turned the water into wine?**

· **What surprising things could Jesus do for you today?**

say ▶ **This was a wonderful surprise! We can make surprises happen, but only Jesus can do real miracles.**

Fill the Jar

Supplies: baby food jars, glue, red tissue paper, paintbrushes

Give children each a jar and a sheet of red tissue paper.

say ▶ **Your jars look like they're filled with clear water, just like the ones the servants filled in our Bible story. Let's change them, sort of like Jesus did!**

Let children paint their jars with glue, then tear pieces of tissue paper and press them to the jar. As the jars "fill up" with "wine," review today's Bible story with the children.

ask ▶ · **How are these jars different from the ones Jesus filled?**

· **Why do you think Jesus can do miracles?**

· **Who can you tell about Jesus' miracles?**

say ▶ **Only Jesus can do miracles like turning water to wine. Whenever you look at your jar, you can remember how powerful Jesus is!**

PRayeRS

Miracles Prayer

Supplies: none

Have the children tell about surprising things that have happened in their families, and have children offer thanks for these miracles. Encourage as many children to pray spontaneously as are willing to do so. End the prayers by saying together, "In Jesus' name, amen!"

Jumping With Thanks

Supplies: none

Have kids start out in a crouching position on the floor, then have them "sprout" up and shout out a prayer of thanks for the miracles God places in our lives, and for the love of Jesus.

PRAY Dear God,

Thank you for your miracles:

For flowers, and trees, and sunshine, too! *(Have kids start crouched down then grow taller bringing their arms up into a circle above their heads to make a sun.)*

Thank you that Jesus is your Son; it's true.

In Jesus' name, amen!

snacks

A Butter Miracle?

Supplies: crackers, plastic knives, a quart-size plastic jar that can be tightly sealed, a half pint of whipping cream, ¼ teaspoon salt

While children are washing their hands, set out crackers, knives, the plastic jar, whipping cream, and salt. Let children each pour a little bit of the whipping cream into the plastic jar until the cream has been completely transferred into the jar, then let the last child add the salt. Secure the lid tightly.

Say Let's see what kind of a surprise we can make from this whipping cream and salt. We should be able to put our surprise on these crackers in just a few minutes. Have the kids sit down in a circle, and begin passing around the jar for the children to shake. It should take about two to three minutes of vigorous shaking for the contents to form a ball of butter. As the children shake the jar, lead them in saying the rhyme below.

RHyMe At a wedding in Cana a long time ago,

Jesus changed water, and wine began to flow.

Jesus' first miracle was now complete.

Jesus does miracles for you and me.

ask • How is our changing cream into butter different from Jesus changing the water into wine?

• How do you feel when something surprising happens?

• How do you think the people at the wedding in Cana felt when Jesus miraculously turned the water into wine?

say ▸ **We changed the cream into butter by shaking it. That's not really a miracle, just a surprising thing that happens. Jesus can do miracles because he is the Son of God.** Invite a child to give thanks for the snacks, then let the children use plastic knives to spread the butter onto their crackers.

Mix and Munch

Supplies: small paper cups, cut-up vegetables such as broccoli and celery, bowl of mayonnaise, bowl of milk, two tablespoons, a bowl of salt, a bowl of dill seasoning, half-teaspoon, craft sticks, paper plates

Set up an assembly line of ingredients for children to change mayonnaise and milk into a dip for their vegetables. Place child-size cups at the beginning of the line. Then place on the table a bowl of mayonnaise with a tablespoon, a bowl of milk with another tablespoon, a small bowl of salt, and a bowl of dill seasoning with a half-teaspoon for the children to use for measuring. At the end of the assembly line, set out craft sticks for stirring.

Have children wash their hands (or use wet wipes). Give each of the children a small plate of cut-up vegetables such as broccoli and celery. Tell kids they will be changing mayonnaise and milk into a dip for the vegetables. Then choose a child to thank God for providing their snack.

Have kids pick up a cup and follow the line along the table for their turn to add each ingredient to their cups. Instruct children to put two spoonfuls of mayonnaise, one spoonful of milk, pick up a tiny bit of salt with their fingers, and then place about a half teaspoon of dill seasoning into their cups. Have kids take a craft stick and their cups back to the table, sit down, and stir the ingredients—changing them from milk and mayonnaise into a dip for their vegetables.

ask ▸ • **What ingredients did you put into your cups?**

• **How did the ingredients you put into your cup change?**

• **What miracles can you ask Jesus to do in your life?**

say ▸ **We made mayonnaise turn into a dip for our vegetables, but Jesus made a real miracle happen—he changed water into wine. Jesus can do miracles.**

SONGS

Jesus Went to a Wedding

Supplies: none

Teach children the words to "Jesus Went to a Wedding" to the tune of "Ninety-Nine Bottles of Pop." Concentrate on the second verse. Some of your older children may be able to learn both verses. This tune has a strong rhythm, so encourage the children to be active by marching around in a circle in time to the song. Reverse directions on the second verse. Repeat the song as many times as possible.

SING
When Jesus went to a wedding one day,
His friends ran out of wine.
So Jesus made some.
He is God's Son.
He helped everything turn out fine.

And Jesus knows when I'm hurting or sad.
He helps me know what to do.
He's the Son of God.
He's Jesus, the Lord.
I know that he cares for me, too!

ASK
· Have you ever made something to eat or drink? What was it?

· Was it hard to do? Why?

SAY
Nothing is hard for Jesus to do. He could even make a special drink out of plain water for his friends. Jesus is the Son of God, and Jesus can do miracles. When you have a friendship with Jesus, you can ask him to help you with the hard things in your life, and he will be with you.

Jesus Clears the Temple to Worship God

Bible Basis:

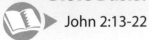 John 2:13-22

Supplies:

Bible, large cardboard "brick" building blocks, stuffed animals, play money, cloth sack

Open your Bible to John 2, and show children the words.

say ▶ **Today's Bible story tells us that worship is important to God. In Jesus' day, people worshipped God in a Temple. It was a very special, holy place like our church. To get ready for our Bible story, let's use these blocks to make a "Temple" right here in our classroom.**

Have kids work together to build a Temple. It can be a simple 3x3-foot square. While kids build, discuss these questions:

ask ▶ • **Why do you think worship is important to God?**

• **How do you think Jesus and the disciples worshipped God?**

• **How do you worship God?**

say ▶ **Worship is important to God because he deserves our thanks and praise. He made us, and he made everything in our world! Jesus and the disciples worshipped in a Temple. They may have sung and prayed like we do today. We worship God in church, but we can also worship God wherever we are. Good job building this Temple! You did fine work. Now close your eyes as I tell you our story. Let's pretend we're back in the days when Jesus was here.** Make sure kids close their eyes.

Make animal sounds as you fill the Temple with the toy animals and play money.

say ▶ **One day, Jesus and the disciples decided to go to the Temple. When Jesus got there, instead of people worshipping God, Jesus found people selling cows, sheep, and doves! Go ahead and open your eyes.** Pause for kids to see their Temple filled with animals and money. **Jesus loves animals, but he was angry because the people were selling them for too much money! So he made all the people who were selling things leave the Temple. Jesus told them, "Get out of here! How dare you turn my Father's house into a store market!"**

Let's clear our Temple, too. Have kids take out the items and place them back in the sack. As they take out each item, have them say, "Get these out of here!" Encourage kids to mend the original Temple if some blocks have tumbled over in the process.

Worship is important to God, and he wants us to worship him with our whole heart.

ask • **What did you think when you opened your eyes and saw your Temple?**

• **How did Jesus feel when he saw the people, money, and animals in the Temple?**

say **You looked surprised when you saw the things that filled your Temple. Jesus could have been surprised, but he also was angry. He wanted the Temple to be a special place to worship the one, true God. God's church shouldn't be crowded with a bunch of people selling stinky animals for more money than they should. Jesus wants us to know that worship is important to God. God made us, and he made everything in the whole world. He loves us. We tell God we love him when we worship him!** On the count of three, have kids say, "We love you, God."

BiBLe eXPeRienCes

Worship Center

Supplies: crepe-paper streamers, CD player, children's music CD, Bible storybooks

Set out the streamers, a CD player and children's CD, and Bible storybooks. Encourage kids to explore a variety of ways to worship God. Have them pray or look at the Bible storybooks and tell one another why they love God. Or they may play worshipful songs from the CD and do creative, worshipful movements to the music using the streamers.

ask • **In what ways do you like to worship God?**

• **How do you feel when you worship God?**

• **How do you think God feels when you worship him?**

say **Worship is important to God. Worship makes us feel good. It feels good to tell God we love him.**

Worship With Music

Supplies: CD player, children's music CD, colorful crepe-paper streamers

Use this listening activity to remind children that we can worship God in many ways. Give each child a bright-colored crepe-paper streamer, and then play a song on the CD. Encourage the children to hold the streamers above their heads as they sway, turn in circles, and make figure-eight motions to the music. Remind the children that worship is important to God. When we worship God, it makes him happy.

ask • **What is your favorite song about Jesus?**

• **How do you feel when you sing at church?**

• **When can we worship God with our singing? playing? dancing?**

CRafts

God's House Is Different

Supplies: prepared envelopes, crayons or markers, stickers

Before class, cut along the diagonal lines of envelopes so that the whole back will open. Give each child one of the envelopes. Tell children that when they open the envelope, it represents the inside of a church building. Have kids draw a cross at the top and center of the open envelope flap. Tell kids to use the stickers and crayons, or other decorating items, to create pictures of what people do inside of a church such as praying, singing, reading the Bible, and talking to others. Now have kids shut the "doors" of the church and draw things on the outside of the church that can distract us from worshipping God, such as money, pets, school, or other worries.

say **In our story, we learned that worship is important to God. The people in Jesus' time had let animals and salesmen into their place of worship. And these people were not being honest. They were selling the animals for too much money. They were not worshipping God with all their heart.**

ask • **What kinds of things keep us from worshipping God today?**

• **How do we fully worship God?**

• **Why is worship important to you?**

say **You can hang your church up to remind you that worshipping God means focusing on God, not on other things that can distract us and take our attention away from God! Worship is important to God!**

Windows for God

Supplies: clear, self-adhesive shelf paper (two 15-inch squares per child); colored tissue paper; four 1x15-inch strips of construction paper per child; scissors; marker; pictures of stained-glass windows

Before class, make a couple of sample "windows." Cut tissue paper into 2-inch squares.

Set the art supplies and the pictures of stained-glass windows on the floor so kids can bow and kneel before God while they create their church windows. Peel the backing off the self-adhesive paper, and lay one sheet sticky-side up in front of each child. Show kids how to make a large square frame with their construction paper strips, and let them place their colored tissue-paper squares inside their frames in any design they choose. When they have completed their windows, write their names on the frames with the marker. Peel the backing off the other sheets of contact paper, lay one over the top of each window, and trim the edges with scissors.

Remind the children that we can worship God as we make beautiful things, such as windows, for him. Worship is important to God.

PRAYERS

Worship Prayer

Supplies: colorful crepe-paper streamers

Have children take turns finishing the prayer, "Jesus, I love you because…" Then after each child's prayer, have all children hold their streamers high, twirl them in circles, and answer, "Let us worship God." Say the following prayer:

PRAY **Lord, thank you for teaching us that worship is important to you. Help us to worship you forever! In Jesus' name, amen.**

snacks

Cleaning Up Snack

Supplies: graham crackers or shortbread cookies, vanilla icing, plastic knives, animal crackers, chocolate coins wrapped in gold foil, paper plates, napkins

Encourage kids to wash their hands before preparing the snack. Ask a volunteer to pray, thanking God for the snack children are about to make and asking him to help them remember to worship God always. Have kids each make a Temple by spreading icing on a cookie or graham cracker. Then have each child fill the "Temple" with a gold coin and some animal cookies. Have kids clear out their Temples as they eat their animal crackers and coins and say, one by one, "Get this out of here!"

Shopping for a Snack

Supplies: small bowls of snacks, sandwich bags, pretend money (strips of colored paper)

Put the snack bowls in different spots around the room. Each snack will be a "store" during this activity.

Have children wash their hands (or use wet wipes). Tell children that some of them are going to be merchants (store people) and pretend to sell today's snack to the other children. Encourage each "merchant" to stand by one of the snack bowls located throughout the classroom. Tell the merchants that they are going to "sell" their snack to the "shoppers." Instruct the merchants to be nice and helpful and to not charge too much. Give each of the other children a sandwich bag and some pretend money (strips of colored paper)—they will be the shoppers. Tell the shoppers to go from location to location, shopping and filling their sandwich bag with snack items they'd like. When the shoppers have finished, they can become the merchants and the other children can shop. When every child has a full bag, kids can pray for their snacks and then enjoy the treat!

ask ▸ • What was it like to shop for today's snack?

• How would you have felt if the store people wouldn't take your money and wouldn't let you have any snack today?

say ▸ In today's Bible story, the merchants charged too much money. The people were there to buy gifts for God, and they didn't have enough money! They were trying to buy these gifts because they wanted to give them to God to worship him. Worship is important to God.

Let Us Worship God

Supplies: none

Lead children in singing, "Let Us Worship God" to the tune of "A Sailor Went to Sea Sea Sea."

SING **Oh, let us worship God, God, God.**

And tell him that we love him so!

Oh, let us worship God, God, God.

And tell him that we love him so!

Repeat this song three times, and each time, encourage kids to choose a new way to move in worship such as kneeling, bowing, waving hands, or twirling in a circle

Jesus Explains Eternal Life to Nicodemus

Bible Basis:

John 3:1-21

Supplies:

Bible, marionette (or person puppet), a piece of black cloth

Have the children sit in a large semicircle so all the children can see. Open your Bible to John 3, and show the children the words.

say ▸ **Today's Bible story tells us that Jesus gives us life in heaven.**

ask ▸ **• How do you act when you're afraid to meet someone?**

say ▸ **There was once a very important man named Nicodemus who was afraid to meet Jesus.** Bring the marionette out, and tell the children that today we will pretend that our marionette puppet is Nicodemus. **Nicodemus had heard about a man named Jesus who could walk on water, heal people, and do all kinds of surprising things!**

Use a different voice for Nicodemus. He should sound sophisticated but humble. **say** ▸ **"Is it true? Could Jesus really be the one sent by God to save us? Maybe…"** Nicodemus thought about it. Bring Nicodemus' hand up and rub his head. **"Maybe…just maybe…Jesus can tell me how I can have life in heaven."** Have Nicodemus point up.

Nicodemus might have said to himself, "I'm afraid someone will see me and make fun of me if I talk to Jesus! I don't want anyone to see me." Move Nicodemus' head side to side. **"Hmm, what can I do so no one will see me?"**

ask ▸ **• What do you do when you want to hide from people?** Let kids stand up and tell or show Nicodemus their response then sit back down.

say ▸ **"Aha! I know!"** Pull Nicodemus' hand up to touch his head. **"I'll put on a black coat and cover my head with a big hood. Then no one will know it's me."**

So late one night, Nicodemus waited until everyone was asleep. He quietly put on his black coat with the hood, and sneaked outside, tiptoeing into the darkness. Drape the black cloth over Nicodemus. The cloth should cover Nicodemus' head but not his eyes. Walk Nicodemus back and forth.

ask ▸ **• Where do you think Nicodemus might have looked for Jesus?**

• How can we talk to Jesus today?

say We can find Jesus right away when we pray. When Nicodemus found Jesus, he told him, "I know you have come from God. You have done such amazing things!"

Jesus knew what question Nicodemus wanted to ask him. Jesus said, "Nicodemus, you need to be born again if you want to see God's kingdom. Only God's Spirit can give you life in heaven."

But Nicodemus didn't understand. Lift Nicodemus' hand up. **"What? How can a grown man, like me, fit back into my mother to be born… again?"**

Jesus told Nicodemus that just like the wind moves without us seeing it (let Nicodemus sway back and forth)**, God's Spirit moves quietly in us when we believe in his Son. He told Nicodemus that God loves all the people in the world so much that God sent Jesus here to earth so that Nicodemus, and everyone else who believes in Jesus, can have life in heaven. All we have to do is believe in Jesus and Jesus will give us life with him in heaven. Isn't that great?**

Have the children form a circle and sit down.

say Nicodemus had many questions for Jesus. He came to Jesus at night so that Jesus would answer his questions. Nicodemus was a very important man. He had a very important job, a lot of money, and a very nice robe. Jesus answered Nicodemus' questions and helped Nicodemus know how to have life in heaven.

ask • What did Jesus come to earth to give us?

• How can you have life in heaven with Jesus?

• What do you believe about Jesus?

say One thing we can believe about Jesus is that he is the Son of God and sits in the high places of heaven with God. Everyone will bow to Jesus because he is the King above every king.

Invite the children to say goodbye to Nicodemus, and then put him away.

CRaftS

God Loves Everyone

Supplies: construction paper, markers, gel pens, stickers

Tell children that God loves the whole world and gave us Jesus. Let them use the supplies to design cards to tell people God loves them. They can draw a world, a picture of Jesus, a cross, or what they think heaven looks like. Encourage kids to give their cards to people they want to tell "God loves the world!"

God Loves the World

Supplies: paper, bowls of blue and green tempera paint, plastic foam balls (cut in half), permanent marker, glue

Provide bowls or trays of blue and green tempera paints, and have each child finger-paint half of a plastic foam ball (after you've written his or her name on it with permanent marker). Be sure the tempera paint is a workable consistency. Encourage the children to paint the ball halves so they look like globes, with green land and blue water. When the paint has dried, have the children glue their globes onto the paper. You might have to wait a while to do this final step.

ask • Why do you think God sent Jesus?

• How do you know that God loves you?

say God loves the world so much that he sent his only Son for us. Jesus came to save us.

Valuable Coupons

Supplies: magazines, scissors, index cards, glue, markers, crayons, glitter, stickers

ask • What are some things we use coupons for?

say That's right. Sometimes, coupons give us free stuff. But we don't always need a coupon. Sometimes people do things for free just because they want to be nice.

ask • What are some things you can do for free to help someone else?

say Today we're going to make coupons to give away to people. These coupons won't be for something to buy. These coupons will be for a chore or a helpful thing you can do for someone, such as cleaning up toys, helping do the dishes, or dusting the furniture.

Help children look through the magazines to find pictures of people doing helpful things for others. Tell children to each cut (or tear) out a picture that represents the thing they would like to do to help someone this week. When kids have finished finding their pictures, have them glue the pictures to index cards. Encourage kids to use markers, crayons, glitter, or stickers to decorate their "coupons."

ask • **Has anyone ever done something free for you?**

• **What does Jesus give us for free?**

say **God sent his Son, Jesus, to set us free, not because of anything we do, but because he loves us and wants us to be with him. Jesus came to save us. We made these coupons today to give to people we love, not because of anything they've done, but because we love them and want to do something for them—for free!**

If you have extra time, let kids make more than one coupon.

A Gift From God

Supplies: T-shaped paper (6 inches wide and 8 inches long, 1 per child), tape, crayons or markers

Give the children each a T-shaped paper, and encourage kids to draw Jesus on the front of it and to decorate the back side to look like a gift. Then show the children how to fold the T-shape, with a fold every two inches, to make a small cube. Make sure the side decorated as a gift is on the outside. Use tape where needed to help the cube stay folded.

Have children hold their gifts and say together, "Jesus wants to give us life in heaven."

ask • **What did you make today?**

• **How did God show us his love?**

• **Who do you know that needs the gift of God's love?**

say **God loved us so much he gave us a special gift, his Son, Jesus.** Tell the children to take their small gifts home to share with their parents, and to tell them that God loved the world so much that he sent Jesus as a gift for everyone.

Games

Hopscotch to Heaven

Supplies: masking tape, gift bows, empty bag

Make a simple hopscotch path on the floor with masking tape. Set a pile of gift bows at the beginning of the hopscotch path and an empty bag at the opposite end of the path.

say ▶ **Let's play a game in which we "save" the gift bows to be used again. One at a time, pick up a gift bow, hop or skip along the hopscotch path, place the bow in the bag, and then hop or skip back. Take turns hopping and skipping until you have saved all the bows in the bag.**

ask ▶ **· How did you save the gift bows in the game?**

· Who did Jesus come to save?

say ▶ **We saved the bows by putting them in a bag to be used again later. And Jesus came to save us. He lived on earth so we'd know how to live, too. He died on a cross for our sins so we can live forever in heaven. Let's tell everyone that Jesus came to save them. Jesus loves us so much!**

Who's in Disguise?

Supplies: paper towels, bedsheet

Give kids large sheets of paper towels, and ask them to hide their faces in the towels. While the children are hiding their eyes, quickly choose a child to be Nicodemus. Stand between the children and "Nicodemus," so the children won't be able to see who Nicodemus is while you're wrapping up him or her in the sheet (in case they peek). Have kids uncover their eyes and try to guess who the person is who is hidden inside the disguise. You could even provide sunglasses or masks so kids can disguise their faces. Remind the children that Nicodemus didn't want to be seen talking to Jesus. But because Nicodemus went to see Jesus, Nicodemus learned that Jesus gives us life in heaven.

ask ▶ **· Have you ever wanted to hide from someone? What did you do?**

· Why was Nicodemus hiding from his friends?

· How did Jesus know who Nicodemus was?

say ▶ **Nicodemus knew that God sent Jesus to teach people about God, and Jesus knew just who Nicodemus was. Jesus told Nicodemus that if he believed in him, Jesus would give him life in heaven. And everyone else who believes in Jesus will have life together in heaven with Jesus, too.**

PRAYERS

Save Us Prayer

Supplies: none

Lead children in singing "Save Us Prayer" as a prayer to the tune of "The Mulberry Bush." Sing the song several times. After each time, ask children to name friends they're praying for or to thank Jesus for saving us.

SING Jesus came to save us, save us, save us!
Jesus came to save us.
God loves the world so!

Close the prayer time by having children say, "In Jesus' name, amen."

SNACKS

Sweet Safety

Supplies: ice-cream scoop, container of warm water, lime sherbet, orange slices, bowls, spoons, blue food coloring

SAY Jesus came to save us. Jesus came to save everyone no matter when they lived or where they lived. We're going to make a globe to remind us of all the people in the world Jesus came to save.

Allow children to take turns dipping the ice cream scoop in warm water and then scooping a round ball of lime sherbet to put in each bowl. You may need to help kids with the scooping. Have the children roll the ball with their spoon to swirl the blue food coloring onto their "globe."

ASK • Why do you think Jesus came to save everyone?

• Who can you tell that Jesus came to save us?

SAY Each of us has a globe to remind us of everyone on earth that Jesus came to save. Now I want you to put orange slices around your globe to make a big orange life preserver—showing that Jesus came to preserve, or care for, us. Jesus came to save all of us!

Newborn Food

Supplies: baby foods that the children will like, such as peaches, peach cobbler, mixed fruits, pears, or apricots; spoons; milk; baby bottles

Have the children wash their hands (or use wet wipes) and then sit down for their snack. Serve the children baby foods. Just for fun, serve milk in baby bottles that you borrowed from some of the moms in your church and sterilized for cleanliness. Remind the children that Jesus gives us life in heaven without having to become a baby all over again.

Choose a child to pray and thank Jesus for providing this fun snack. Your children will delight in this special opportunity to pretend to be babies again.

The Missing Rhyme

Supplies: none

Say the following rhyme, but don't say the rhyming words in brackets. Do the motions suggested, and have the children guess the rhyming words from the motions. Tell them the word if they can't guess it.

 A cake without frosting is really quite sad. *(Pretend to lick frosting off a cake.)*

A clock without numbers would make people [mad]**.** *(Tap "wristwatch" and scowl.)*

A cat without fur would get mighty [cold]**.** *(Hold yourself and shiver.)*

Eggs without shells would be too hard to [hold]**.** *(Cup hands.)*

And so it is true; I feel it in my [heart]**.** *(Put hands over heart.)*

If Jesus is missing, I don't have the best part. *(Wiggle hands and fly them away from your heart.)*

So, Lord, send us Jesus to live deep inside us. *(Point to heart.)*

We love him; we need him to be right beside us. *(Hug yourself and smile.)*

"God Loves You" Rhyme

As you help your children say this active rhyme, remind them that Jesus gives us life in heaven.

RHyMe ▶ **God loves the world.** *(Make a circle with both hands.)*
God loves you. *(Point to others.)*
God gave Jesus *(point up to heaven)*
For me and you. *(Point to self then to a friend.)*

God loves the world. *(Make a circle with both hands.)*
God loves you. *(Point to others.)*
Believe in Jesus *(point to your heart)*,
And go to heaven, too. *(Walk in place.)*

Jesus Talks With a Samaritan Woman

Bible Basis:

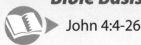

John 4:4-26

Supplies:

Bible, picture or drawing of a well, bucket, picture of Jesus, tape, pictures of different kinds of drinks

Before class, tape the picture of Jesus to the bottom of the bucket. Put the pictures of drinks into the bucket. Open your Bible to John 4, and show the children the words.

say ▸ **Today's Bible story tells us that Jesus brings life. There was once a woman who was very thirsty. She went to the well to get some water. A well is a deep hole that people put buckets into so they can bring water up to drink. The well might have looked something like this one.** Show the picture of the well. **Jesus was standing by the well, and he knew the woman was thirsty.**

ask ▸ • **What do you drink when you feel thirsty?**

Pass around the bucket, and let each child pull out a picture of something to drink. Identify each picture with the children, and then have the child put the picture back into the bucket and pass it on to the next child. Ask which drinks are hot and which are cold. Ask which drinks children like the best and why.

say ▸ **These are all good things to drink. But drinking these things would not fill you up forever. You would feel thirsty again soon.**

Jesus knew that the woman at the well was sad and she needed more than a drink to fill her up. I wonder what the woman at the well found that filled her up with life forever? Pull the picture of Jesus from the bottom of the bucket. **Jesus gave her new life!**

ask ▸ • **How do you feel when you're really thirsty and you finally get something to drink?**

• **How do you think the woman felt when she was tired and Jesus gave her a fresh new life?**

say ▸ **Jesus gave the woman at the well much more than just water. Jesus gave her new life. The woman at the well learned that if she had Jesus, she would always be alive. She would be able to know him and live with him forever. The woman was very happy to know that Jesus brings life, so she went to tell everyone she knew! Then they wanted to know Jesus, too. They wanted the life that Jesus could give them.**

BIBLE EXPERIENCES

Water "Taste Test"

Supplies: cups, warm water, ice, cold water, lemonade mix

Set out several cups of warm water, several cups of ice water, and cups of water with the lemonade mix added. Ask each child to close his or her eyes and taste the three cups of water. Have kids describe the differences between the cups of water. Is the liquid warm, cold, sweet, sour?

ask
- Which drink did you like best? Why?
- What did Jesus give the woman at the well that was better than water?

say Jesus gave the woman at the well something extra special. He gave her new life. This means that she could be with Jesus forever.

ask
- How do you think the woman felt after Jesus gave her new life?

say The woman was happy and excited when she learned that Jesus brings life. She went to tell everyone she knew the wonderful news!

Watering Trip

Supplies: small watering cans or cups

Take children on a "watering trip." Provide small watering cans or cups, and encourage children to water plants inside and outside the church. Point out that water helps the plants to live and Jesus brings life to boys and girls by being with them forever. Be sure to obtain permission for the adventure from your children's parents and the ministry director.

PRAYERS

New Life Celebration

Supplies: none

Ask children to sit in a circle. Remind them that Jesus gives life. Have children practice jumping up to show excitement about life. Then lead children in popping up one at a time to say the following sentence prayer:

 Thank you, Jesus, for giving me eternal life. In Jesus' name, amen.

SONGS

"I Like Living" Rhyme

Supplies: none

As you teach the children this rhyme, do the motions with lots of enthusiasm to emphasize what a great life Jesus gives. Invite the children to stand up before you begin.

 I like to sing and laugh and play. *(Hold hands with a friend, and turn around in a circle.)*

I like living every day! *(Continue turning.)*

Jesus makes life what it is. *(Throw up your arms exuberantly.)*

He is mine and I am his. *(Point up, point to your chest, and then point up again.)*

Jesus Blesses the Children

Bible Basis:

 Mark 10:13-16

Supplies:

Bible

Before you begin, assign parts so each child can pretend to be a character in the story. One child should be Jesus. Other roles might be disciples, adults, and children in the crowd.

Open your Bible to Mark 10, and show children the words.

 **say** **Today's Bible story teaches us that we are important to Jesus.**

The Bible tells us that Jesus was talking to many people. Have the child playing Jesus pretend to talk to the "disciples" and "adults."

Some of the mommies and daddies from the town brought their children to see Jesus. Have the children pretending to be mommies, daddies, and children spread out around the room and then walk toward "Jesus" and sit down to listen.

Jesus was very busy healing the sick people and telling others about God's love for them. There were many children there that day, too. They might have even been laughing and playing and running around just as you like to do. Have the students who are pretending to be children play behind the "crowds of people" listening to Jesus.

Some people brought their children to Jesus, but the disciples were worried that the children might bother Jesus. So the disciples told the people to keep the children back and keep them quiet. But the children wanted to see Jesus. Have the kids playing the parts of parents and children try to get to Jesus. Have the disciples block their way.

Jesus heard what was happening and wasn't very happy. He told the disciples to let people bring their children to him. Jesus told his disciples that the children were important to him. Then Jesus called the children to him. He picked up each and every child and blessed them all. Have the child pretending to be Jesus motion the children to come to him and give each child a hug. After the children have received their hugs, have them sit in a circle.

ask • Who makes you feel important?

• Why do you think Jesus thinks you're special?

say It can make us feel good to know that we're important to Jesus.

BiBLe eXPeRieNCeS

Who's Important?

Supplies: small cross made out of card stock

Have kids sit in a circle with their hands behind them. Give the cross to a child, and have him or her walk around the outside of the circle asking three times, "Who's important to Jesus?" Then have the child put the cross in another child's hands. That child should hold the cross up and shout out, "I am important to Jesus!" Go around the circle and have kids take turns telling the child with the cross, "Jesus loves you, [child's name]." Then the child with the cross becomes the one to circle around the others. Encourage kids to give the cross to a new child each time. Continue until everyone has had a turn and has been affirmed.

ask • How did you feel when the cross came to you?

• How can you show others they are important to Jesus, too?

say You are so important to Jesus that he died on a cross for your sins. Because Jesus loves you so much, you and everyone else who loves Jesus get to live in heaven forever. Jesus wants you to remember that you are important to him. Let's remember to tell others how much Jesus loves them.

Important People

Supplies: footstool, stuffed animal

Place the footstool at the front of the room, and have the children sit close together on the floor in front of the stool. Have children take turns standing on the footstool, holding a stuffed animal, and being the important person. As each child takes his or her turn, have the rest of the children say, "You are important to Jesus." Have the important child respond by saying, "I am important to Jesus" and giving the stuffed animal a big hug.

ask · How did you feel when you were the important person on the footstool?

· What can you do to show others that they are important to Jesus?

say You are important to Jesus. Jesus loves you, and Jesus wants you to feel special and loved. We can tell others that they are important to Jesus, too. Jesus loves everyone in the whole world!

CRafts

Come to Jesus

Supplies: paper, gel pens, paper fasteners, paper "arms," scissors

Distribute the paper, and have kids write their names on them. Set out gel pens, and paper fasteners.

Have kids draw pictures on their pages to look like themselves. Then have kids attach Jesus "arms" to their paper with paper fasteners. Make the arms tuck around the child's picture so it looks as if Jesus has his arm around him or her.

ask · Why does Jesus want us to come to him?

· How can we come to Jesus today?

say In our story, people brought children to Jesus so he could bless them. Jesus wants us to come to him, too. We can come to Jesus when we pray, worship, and talk with other Christians. We are important to Jesus, and he wants to be close to us always!

Hands of Love

Supplies: construction paper hearts, accordion-folded construction paper, construction paper "hands," crayons or markers, glue

say Jesus wanted the little kids to come to him, and Jesus wants you to come to him, too! You are important to Jesus! Let's make a craft that shows how Jesus touched the children and blessed them.

Give each child a construction paper heart, a piece of accordion-folded construction paper, and a construction paper hand that you prepared before class. Encourage kids to draw pictures of children on their hearts. If you have extra time, let kids look through old magazines and tear out pictures of children to glue onto their hearts. When kids have finished drawing children, help them each glue one end of the accordion-folded construction paper onto the back of the paper hand and then glue the other end of the accordion-folded paper onto the picture of children so the hand is bobbing over the children.

ask • **How do you feel when someone gives you a hug or high five?**

• **How do you think the children felt when Jesus wanted to bless them?**

• **How are you important to Jesus?**

say **Your picture shows that Jesus loves and blesses all the children in the world. You can take your craft home to help you remember that you are important to Jesus.**

PRayeRS

"Important" Prayer

Supplies: card stock cross

Lead children in the following prayer. At the appropriate time during the prayer, pass the cross around the circle and have each child say his or her name.

PRay **Thank you, Jesus, that you love us. It makes us so happy to know that each one of us in this circle is important to you.** Pass the cross around the circle and have each child say his or her name. **Help us love others the way you love us. Help us tell others they are important to you, too. In Jesus' name, amen.**

"Thank You, Jesus"

Supplies: none

Have children act out the following prayer as they say the words with you.

PRay **Thank you, Jesus** *(lift both arms up to heaven),*
For calling me important. *(Give yourself a hug.)*
In Jesus' name, amen.

snacks

An Important Ingredient

Supplies: sandwich cookies, unsweetened lemonade, sweetened lemonade, cups, napkins

Remind children to wash their hands or use wet wipes. Choose a child to pray and thank God for providing the snack.

Serve the children sandwich cookies, and discuss the importance of each ingredient in the cookie. Pour a small amount of unsweetened lemonade into each child's cup. Wait for the children's responses.

ask • **What important ingredient is this lemonade missing?**

say **This lemonade has no sugar in it! Let's try some lemonade that has sugar.** Add sweetened lemonade to each cup so children can enjoy the taste.

ask • **Why is sugar important to lemonade?**

• **Why are you important to Jesus?**

say **Just as sugar is important to lemonade, you are important to Jesus.**

songs

"Let the Children Come" Action Rhyme

Supplies: none

Say the following rhyme to the children and do the motions. Encourage the children to join you as they learn the words. On the third line, call a child's name, and have him or her come sit in your lap. Repeat the rhyme until each child has had a turn. Remind children that they are important to Jesus.

Rhyme **The disciples said, "Stay back. Jesus is a very busy man."** *(Shake finger back and forth, then hold hand in front of you.)*

Jesus said, "Come close, for I have a special plan. *(Speak in a gentle voice and beckon.)*

Come, [child's name], sit upon my knee *(have child sit in your lap),*

For you are important to me." *(Give child a hug.)*

Jesus Tells About a Good Samaritan

Bible Basis:

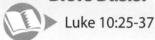 Luke 10:25-37

Supplies:

Bible, tissues, "gold" coins, bandages

Open your Bible to Luke 10, and show the children the words.

say **Today's Bible story teaches us that God wants us to care for others. Our story has many people and a donkey in it, and you'll get to do some motions during the story! Let's practice being the different characters in the story.**

First, let's pretend to be the hurt man. Can you groan or cry like you've been hurt? Encourage children to groan and cry.

Now let's practice being donkeys. Hold your hands beside your head to be donkey ears. Show children how to make donkey ears.

The main person in our story is the good Samaritan. He's a very kind man. Give children each a tissue, and show them how to dab each other's arms as if cleaning a sore.

Next is the innkeeper. He has money in his hand. Give each child a gold coin. **Can you hold your money out like the innkeeper?** Show children how to hold out the money in their open palms.

The last people are robbers. Robbers are mean people who take things that don't belong to them. Can you make a mean face? Encourage children to pretend to take things from others.

Now let's act out the story together. I'll tell what happened, and you can help me by doing the actions during our Bible story.

Once there was a man who was traveling on a road. Let's pretend he is riding on his donkey. Lead children in making donkey ears. **There were robbers hiding in the bushes along the road. They were mean.** Make a mean face with the children. **The robbers took the man's money and his donkey and hurt him.** Groan or cry with the children.

The hurt man lay there for a long time, and no one helped him. Two people walked by the hurt man and refused to help. They were afraid that they would be hurt also, so they quickly walked by him on the other side of the road. Let's count the two men...1...2. Lead the children in holding up one finger at a time and counting to 2.

Then the good Samaritan came by and saw the hurt man. Lead the children in gently dabbing each other's arms as if cleaning a sore. **The good Samaritan wanted to take care of him, but he saw that the hurt man needed more help than he could give. So the good Samaritan put the hurt man on his donkey and took the hurt man to an inn where he could get well.** Have the children make donkey ears. **The good Samaritan gave the innkeeper money so the innkeeper could take care of the hurt man until he could come back.** Lead children in holding out the gold coins. **The good Samaritan and the innkeeper helped the hurt man get better.** Have children put the coins in a pile in the center of the circle.

ask • **How do you think the good Samaritan felt when he saw the hurt man?**

• **Have you ever seen someone get hurt? What happened?**

• **Did you help the hurt person? How did you feel then?**

say The good Samaritan took care of the hurt man and helped him get better. God wants us to care for others, too. Here are some bandages. Hold up the bandages. **We can use bandages to help someone who is hurt.**

ask • **What are some other ways that we can help people?**

BiBLe eXPeRienceS

A Two-Handed Task

Supplies: bandannas folded into simple slings

Have each child remove one shoe and place one arm in a bandanna sling. Encourage children to try to put their shoes back on using only one hand. Then have children help each other to put their shoes back on. Tell helpers they can take off the sling to help their friend.

ask • **How did it feel to try to put your shoe on with only one hand?**

• **How did it feel when someone helped you?**

• **How do you think the hurt man felt when the good Samaritan helped him?**

say Just like you might have needed help to put your shoe back on, the hurt man needed help. The good Samaritan helped the hurt man and took care of him. God wants us to care for others, too.

Helping Hand

Supplies: paper, crayons, adhesive bandages

Show children how to place one hand on a piece of paper and trace around it with a crayon. Some children might need help doing this. You may also want to put kids in pairs and have one child trace around the fingers of the second child. Tell kids that this is a "helping" hand. Children will take their helping hands home, and each day they do something helpful for someone else, kids can color something special on the hand pictures. Kids may want to color the fingernails or draw a picture on the palm of the hand. Then have each child place an adhesive bandage on his or her own hand as a reminder to help someone today.

ask
- What are some ways you can help someone this week?
- Who are some people you can help this week?
- How do you feel when you help someone?

say God wants us to care for others because that's how we share God's love. When we meet again next week, I will ask you how you helped other people this week. You can tell me some of the ways you were God's helping hand!

PRayeRS

Action Prayer

Supplies: none

Gather the children into a circle. Remind children that Jesus wants us to care for others. Say the following rhyming prayer and do the motions together.

PRay Help me, Jesus, to be kind *(point to heaven on "Jesus"),*
To care for others when I find *(point to others)*
That they have need of love and prayers. *(Fold your hands in prayer.)*
Help me be the one who cares. *(Point to yourself.)*
In Jesus' name, amen.

"Serving Others" Snacks

Supplies: small cups, pretzels, heart candies, bowls

After children have washed their hands, have the kids sit in a circle. Choose a child to pray, thanking God for his love and for providing the snacks. Have kids serve others as they would want to be served. Set out bowls of pretzels and heart candies, and let the children take turns filling small cups with a mixture of the snack items. Remind kids that Jesus says love each other. Instruct children to take turns around the circle serving the snack to the child who is sitting on the left, and have children tell the friend that they love him or her.

Put on a Happy Face

Supplies: round crackers, cream cheese, raisins, plastic knives, paper plates

Have children wash their hands (or use wet wipes) and then sit down. Give each child a paper plate. Encourage children to create snacks for each other by spreading the cream cheese onto a cracker. Have them use raisins to make happy faces. Explain that when we care for each other, it makes us all feel happy. Have children show their care for each other by giving their snacks to friends.

ask
- **How does it feel to make a snack for a friend?**
- **How did it feel when your friend gave you a snack?**
- **What are some other ways we can care for each other?**

say **The good Samaritan wanted to take care of the hurt man. It must have made him feel happy to care for the man. Caring for others will make us happy, too. God wants us to care for others.** Invite one child to pray for the snack.

SONGS

"Kindly Caring" Rhyme

Supplies: none

As you teach the children this active rhyme, remind them that God wants us to care for others.

 God wants me to help and share *(hug yourself)*

And show others that I care. *(Hold your arms out to the sides.)*

Caring for the great and small *(hold your hand up high and then bring it down low),*

Jesus loves them one and all. *(Throw a two-handed kiss to heaven.)*

Jesus Heals a Blind Man

Bible Basis:

Mark 10:46-52

Supplies:

Bible

Open your Bible to Mark 10, and show the children the words.

 **say** **Today's Bible story teaches us that Jesus cares for us.**

One day Jesus and his disciples were very tired. They wanted to rest, but many people still wanted to see Jesus. A blind man named Bartimaeus was sitting by the road begging for money. He called so loudly to get Jesus' attention that people told him to be quiet. Have the children pretend to be Bartimaeus and call out to get Jesus' attention.

When Bartimaeus heard that Jesus was coming his way, he began to shout louder, "Jesus, help me! Jesus, have mercy on me and help me!" Have the children repeat these words and call out louder.

Group the children in pairs. Have the partners take turns closing their eyes and repeating the words to show how they would get Jesus to hear them. Then have one partner pretend to be Jesus while the other pretends to be the blind man, and encourage the "blind" partner to close his or her eyes and move around to find "Jesus." Then have kids reverse roles.

ask • **How did it feel to try to find someone when you had your eyes closed?**

say **Some of the people told Bartimaeus to be quiet, but he called out even louder, "Jesus, help me! Jesus, take care of me." Jesus heard the man and stopped. He told the people to bring Bartimaeus to him. Jesus asked, "Why do you call me? What do you want me to do for you?" Bartimaeus told Jesus that he wanted to see. Jesus cared so much for the man, and all of a sudden Bartimaeus could see!**

Have the children return to their partners. Have one child in each pair pretend to be Jesus. Have the other child in each pair close his or her eyes to pretend to be blind Bartimaeus. Have the children pretending to be Jesus say, "Open your eyes and see." Have the children pretending to be Bartimaeus act out the excitement of being able to see for the first time. Have the children switch roles. Then bring them back to the large group.

ask ► • What do you think Bartimaeus may have done after Jesus helped him see again?

say ► Bartimaeus was so happy that Jesus made him see that he followed Jesus down the road.

BiBLe eXPeRiences

The Caring Path

Supplies: blindfold; "obstacles" for a course, such as chairs, toys, and piles of blocks

Blindfold one child at a time. Have another child take the blindfolded child by the hand and lead him or her through the obstacle course you created. As kids walk through the course, remind them that friends care for each other and want to help each other.

ask ► • How did other people help Bartimaeus?

• How did your friend help you when he or she led you through the obstacle course?

• How does Jesus care for us when we need help?

say ► In our story we learned that Jesus cared for blind Bartimaeus. When we ask Jesus for help, he will help us because Jesus cares for us, too.

Blindfolded Builders

Supplies: blocks, blindfolds

Lead children to an area where you have blocks set up and plenty of space for kids to work and build. Place a blindfold around each child's head, and let kids try to build things while blindfolded. (It's OK if some children don't want to be blindfolded.) Remind kids that today's Bible story was about a man who was blind and couldn't see.

CRafts

Worship Art

Supplies: disposable (solid color) plastic tablecloth, masking tape, paint smocks, tempera paint, paper, CD player, children's music CD

Cover a table with a solid-color, plastic, disposable tablecloth. Use masking tape to mark off each child's painting area to match the size of the paper you are using. You'll also need tempera paint and one sheet of paper for each child. If you don't have a sink in your room, have a tub of warm soapy water and paper towels nearby.

say ▶ **Jesus shows he cares for us by giving us the world and all of its beautiful creations, our families, our friends, and our wonderful church. Let's use our eyes, hands, and hearts to worship Jesus and to show him our thankfulness for his care.**

Play a children's CD in the background as children work. Have children put on paint smocks. Put paint on the plastic tablecloth, and have kids rub it around with their hands to make pretty designs of things they're thankful for, such as family, friends, a cross, and so on. When kids finish, have them wash their hands. Give each one a sheet of paper to press onto his or her paint design. Then let the designs dry in a designated area.

ask ▶ • **How does it make you feel to know that Jesus cares for you?**

• **Who can you tell that Jesus cares for him or her?**

say ▶ **Let's tell everyone that Jesus cares for us.**

Heartfelt Care

Supplies: large construction paper hearts with hole punched at the top, crayons or markers, googly eyes, glue, strips of construction paper (four per child), yarn

Give each child one of the hearts you prepared before class. Encourage children to use the crayons, markers, and googly eyes to decorate the hearts and make them look like faces. Show children how to fold the four strips of paper like fans or accordions and then glue two of the strips to the heart as legs and two of the strips as arms. Next, help each child thread one end of the yarn through the hole at the top of the heart. Tie the string in a bow at the top. Tell children they can hang their heart somewhere in their room as a reminder that Jesus loves and cares for every single person in the world.

ask ▶ • **What do you see when you close your eyes?**

• **What do you see when you open your eyes?**

• **Why do you think we put eyes on the hearts we just decorated?**

say Today's Bible story was about a man who could not see with his eyes but he believed in his heart that Jesus cared for him and could help him. Jesus cares for us, too! Every time you see this heart, remember that Jesus cares for you.

Games

Healing Tag

Supplies: CD player, children's music CD

Play some music on the CD. Have children sit in a circle and put their hands over their eyes so they can't see. Choose one child to be the "Tagger." Tell children to say in quiet voices, "Jesus, help me" over and over as the Tagger walks around the inside of the circle. Stop the music, and encourage the Tagger to move to the child he or she is standing in front of and take the child's hands away from his or her eyes. The newly "healed" child can jump up and say, "Thank you! I can see." That child should then become the next Tagger. Try to stop the music when the Tagger is behind a child who hasn't been selected before. Continue playing until all the children have had a chance to be the Tagger and to be "healed."

ask • How did you feel when you couldn't see?

• How do you think the blind man felt when he could not see?

• How can Jesus care for you?

say Jesus cared for the blind man so much that he helped him see. When the man called to Jesus for help, he believed that Jesus would help him. Just like the blind man who called out to Jesus, we can call out to Jesus, too. We can call out to Jesus by praying because Jesus cares for us.

Happy-Sad Prayers

Supplies: sheet of paper, pencil

Have kids take turns telling you about things they need from Jesus, such as help finding new friends, healing for a sick relative, courage to tell others about Jesus, and so on. Write the requests on a paper. Then have kids crouch down with their eyes closed, looking sad, as you say each prayer request followed by the phrase "help us remember." Then have kids smile, jump up, and say together "Jesus cares for us."

PRay **Dear Jesus,**

[Prayer request] **Help us remember "Jesus cares for us."**

[Prayer request] **Help us remember "Jesus cares for us."**

Continue for all the prayer requests. Then have kids say the following line with you.

In Jesus' name, amen.

- -

"Take Care of Me" Prayer

Supplies: none

Sing this prayer to the tune of "Old MacDonald Had a Farm." Then close by saying together, "In Jesus' name, amen."

PRay **Jesus, please take care of me,**
J-E-S-U-S.
Jesus, please take care of me,
J-E-S-U-S.
Thank you, God, for loving me.
Jesus, please take care of me.
O, Jesus, please take care of me,
J-E-S-U-S.

Bartimaeus Snack

Supplies: flavored rice cakes, cans of squirt cheese, slices of summer sausage, napkins

Ask kids to wash their hands before they prepare their snacks.

Encourage kids to retell the Bible story to one another as they design their Bartimaeus snack. Have them squirt cheese on rice cakes and design Bartimaeus' hair, nose, and mouth. When they get to the part of the story in which Bartimaeus can see, have them add two slices of sausage to the rice cakes for eyes.

Ask a volunteer to say a prayer to thank Jesus for caring for Bartimaeus and for caring for us, too. Then enjoy!

- -

What Can I See?

Supplies: miscellaneous snacks such as pretzels, square cheese crackers, oyster crackers, and so on; large bowl; paper cup

Have children wash their hands or use wet wipes. Create a snack mix in a large bowl. Use a paper cup to serve the children.

ask
- **What shapes do you see in your snack?**
- **How do you think Bartimaeus ate food if he couldn't see it?**

say **Bartimaeus couldn't see until Jesus healed him. Just as Jesus cared for and healed Bartimaeus, Jesus cares for us, too.** Choose a child to thank God for the snack, and then let them eat and enjoy!

Jesus Notices a Widow's Giving

Bible Basis:

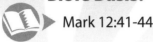

Mark 12:41-44

Supplies:

Bible, "sad" card (with the word sad and a sad face), "mad" card (with the word mad and a mad face), "glad" card (with the word glad and a glad face), fake gold coins (1 per child), bowl or offering plate

Open your Bible to Mark 12, and show children the words.

Say ▶ Today's Bible story teaches us that God wants us to give our best.

Choose three children, and have each child hold one of the "Sad," "Mad," or "Glad" cards.

Say ▶ This Bible story starts in a sad way. Have the class point to the sad face while the child holds it up high. **But I think you'll like the way it ends!** Glad face.

It's a story about a widow. A widow is a woman whose husband has died. Sad face. **She was sad to lose her husband because she loved him very much, but she loved God, too, and knew that God would take care of her.** Glad face.

This widow did not have very much money because she did not have a job. Sad face. **But she still knew that she should give money to the Temple, which was her church.** Glad face.

The widow didn't have much money to give, but she didn't care what other people thought because she knew that God loves a cheerful giver. Glad face.

One day, she went to the Temple to give her money to God. All she had was a couple of coins, not nearly as much as she wanted to give to God. Sad face. **But it was OK! God wants us to give our best, and this was the best that she could give.** Glad face.

There was someone else at the Temple that day who was also giving money to God. He had a lot of money, so when he dropped his money in the box, it made a BIG noise! Drop the gold coins on the floor.

Everyone in the whole Temple turned to see what this man was doing. Some people might have gotten angry that their money didn't make as much noise dropping in the box. Mad face.

Then it was the widow's turn. She took her coin and put it quietly in the box. There was no big noise. No one saw what she gave to God. Sad face. **But Jesus was at the Temple that day, and he saw her**. Glad face. **And that's all that mattered.**

Have each child pick up one of the coins you've dropped on the floor.

say ▶ **God wants us to give our best, and it's OK if our best is only one coin.** Pass around the offering plate or bowl, and have the children put in their gold coins one at a time.

ask ▶ **· How did you feel when you gave your only coin to God?**

Have the children point to the sad, mad, or glad face as they give their answers.

· Do you think the widow felt the same way you did? Why or why not?

· What are some things you can give to God?

CRafts

Bank on It

Supplies: newspaper, clean baby food jars, silver and gold tissue paper, paintbrushes, shallow bowls filled halfway with white glue

Cover a table with newspaper, and set out baby food jars, tissue paper, paintbrushes, and three or four shallow bowls filled halfway with white glue.

Show children how to make "stained-glass" banks by tearing tissue paper into small pieces and gluing the pieces to the outside of the jars. Instruct children to brush the glue all over the outside of the baby food jars, and then press the small pieces of tissue paper to the sides to make the stained-glass effect. Set the jars aside to dry.

ask ▶ **· How did the poor woman give her best to God?**

· How do you think God feels when we give our best to him?

say ▶ **Take your banks home to help you remember the poor woman who did her best and gave all she had to live on to God. Save money in your banks, and then give it to the church or to some people you know who need it. Remember, God wants us to give our best.**

Open Hands

Supplies: paper, pencils, flesh-tone crayons, plastic or candy coins, glue

Distribute the paper. Have each child place a hand on the page and use a pencil to trace carefully around it. Have kids color their hands in flesh-tone crayons. Then have them glue the coins onto their paper hands.

ask
- **Why does God want us to give?**
- **What would be hard for you to give away?**

say Our open hands remind us to keep giving to God. He'll be pleased as we learn to open our hands and give because God wants us to give our best.

Games

Together-Giving Game

Supplies: CD player, children's music CD

Play a round of Musical Chairs. Have each child walk around the chairs and then find a seat once the music has stopped. After the first round, explain to the children that the rules are changing. Take away one chair. Explain that the next time you stop the music, instead of trying to get chairs for themselves, all the children are going to work together to give a seat to everyone, even though there will not be enough chairs. Encourage children to share their seats, to push chairs together to make larger chairs, or even to sit in each other's laps! Let kids come up with their own creative ideas to give a seat to everyone. Each round after the music stops, continue taking away another chair until it's impossible for all the kids to fit on the remaining chairs.

ask
- **How hard would it have been to just give a chair to one of your friends?**
- **What was it like to work with your friends to give everyone a seat?**
- **Would it mean more to you if someone gave you an old toy he or she had laying around the house or if someone gave you a brand-new shiny toy that he or she worked hard to give you? Why?**

say God gave us the very best gift of all when he sent his own Son, Jesus, to earth. And when we give to others, he wants us to work hard at giving our best, too. God wants us to give our best. You did a great job working together with your friends, giving your best together to make sure everyone could have fun playing the game. Good job!

PRAYERS

Coin Prayer

Supplies: offering basket, pennies

Put an offering basket in the center of the circle, and give each person a penny.

 Let's pray and tell God that we love him and that we will give him our best this week. We'll go around the circle. When it's your turn, drop your penny in the offering basket, and tell God how you will give your best to him this week.

Have each child pray: "Dear God, I love you so much, I will give you my best by _____." Examples are "being nice to my younger brother," "asking my friend to church," "giving snacks to my neighbor," "singing nicely at church," or "saying my prayers each night." When everyone has prayed, close by praying:

 God, we love you very much. We are happy to give you our best, just like the poor woman who gave you her coins did.

In Jesus' name, amen.

Action Prayer

Supplies: paper, crayons or markers, basket

Ask each child to name the best thing he or she could give to God. Have the child draw a picture of the item on a piece of paper, or write the name of it on the paper for the child. Gather the children in a circle, and ask them to put their papers in a basket one at a time. Remind kids that this is what they're giving to Jesus; he is watching and is pleased with them. As they drop their papers into the basket, have the children repeat this prayer or one of their own.

 **Dear Lord,**
I want to give you my best.
I give you [child describes what is on the paper].
Please help me be a cheerful giver.
In Jesus' name, amen.

snacks

Banana Coins

Supplies: paper plates, plastic knives, bananas, bowl, chocolate sprinkles

Have children wash their hands, and provide clean table space for children to prepare their snack. Distribute a paper plate and a plastic knife to each child.

say In today's lesson we heard about a woman who gave two small coins as an offering to God. It was not a lot of money, but it was all she had. She knew that God wants us to give our best. And that's what she did!

Cut a 1-inch piece off of each banana half and distribute the pieces to the children. Save the remaining bananas for use after the discussion. Show children how to peel the banana piece and slice it into two round sections shaped like coins. Have children count their two slices and put them into a bowl like the woman who put her two coins into the offering box. Remove the bowl from the children's sight. (Discard these pieces that have been handled.)

ask • How would you feel if you could share your banana snack with Jesus?

• What are other ways you can give your best to God?

• How do you feel when you give your best to God?

say The woman had only two small coins, but she wanted to give her best to God. She gave God all she had, knowing that God would always take care of her. God will take care of us and give us what we need, too. God gives us so much, and that's why God wants us to give our best to him.

Give children the rest of their banana halves, and encourage them to cut and count their pieces. Put chocolate sprinkles on the paper plates, and show kids how to dip their banana pieces in the sprinkles. Ask a volunteer to say a prayer of thanks for the snack they enjoyed and for all that God gives us.

Neat-to-Eat Give-Away Treat

Supplies: paper lunch bags, stickers, large mixing bowl, cheese crackers, raisins, candy pieces, large spoon, ladle, paper plates

Encourage the children to decorate lunch bags with stickers and then make a snack mix together to put inside the bags. Have the children take turns putting the following items into a large mixing bowl: cheese crackers, raisins, and candy pieces. Then have them take turns stirring the mix and using a ladle to scoop some snack mix into their bags. Give each child a plateful to snack on. Let the children experience the joy of giving by taking their snack mixes home to their families.

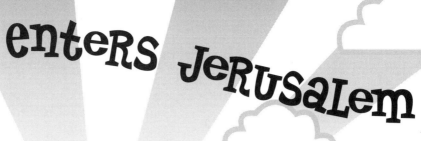

Jesus Enters Jerusalem

Bible Basis:

▶ Matthew 21:1-11

Supplies:

Bible, paper palm branches (made before class)

Have children sit in a circle. Open your Bible to Matthew 21, and show the children the words. Give each child a paper palm branch.

say ▶ **Today's Bible story tells us that Jesus deserves our praise.**

When Jesus lived on earth, some people praised him by waving palm branches and shouting, "Hosanna!" Do you think you can jump up and wave your palm branch every time I say "hosanna"? Let's try it. Hosanna! Encourage children to jump up, wave their palm branches, and then sit back down.

The people were excited; a parade was coming! This wasn't just any parade—the celebration was for Jesus! Jesus was riding into Jerusalem on a donkey. As Jesus passed by, the people shouted, "Hosanna!" Pause for the children to jump up and wave their palm branches and then sit back down.

Many of the people knew that Jesus was a very special person. They thought he was special because he did so many good things and because they had been waiting for him to come for a long time. The people took off their coats and spread them on the ground for the donkey to walk on. Then they shouted, "Hosanna!" Pause for the waving of palm branches. **The people waved their palm branches and again shouted, "Hosanna!"** Have children jump up and wave the palms and then sit back down.

Someone asked, "Who is that?" The people answered, "This is Jesus, who comes in the name of the Lord. Hosanna!" Have children jump up and wave the palms and then sit back down.

ask • **How do you think the people felt as Jesus rode into town?**

• **Why did the people shout "Hosanna!" and wave the palm branches?**

say ▶ **The people celebrated and praised Jesus because he was so special. We want to praise Jesus, too. Jesus deserves our praise.**

BiBLe eXPeRiences

Hosanna Hop

Supplies: jackets, paper palm branches

Ask the children to help you prepare the "road" for Jesus by spreading the jackets along a pretend path. Encourage children to take turns trotting or galloping down the road. While one child is taking a turn going down the road pretending to be Jesus, encourage the rest of the children to line up beside the road with their palm branches. Have kids wave their palm branches and shout, "Hosanna!"

ask • How do you think the people felt as they were praising Jesus?

• How does it make you feel to praise Jesus?

say Jesus is holy. He is the Son of God. He deserves all honor and glory. Jesus deserves our praise.

CRafts

Praise Castanets

Supplies: 1½x8-inch strips of cardboard, 2 soda caps per child, glue, markers

Give each child a strip of cardboard that you prepared before class. Encourage kids to decorate one side of the cardboard with markers. Help kids fold the strip in half and then glue the soda caps inside (top side down), one inch from the ends of the cardboard strip. Allow a short drying time. Show children how to hold the folded cardboard between their thumb and four fingers to tap the caps together, then release it. As they play their castanets, have them sing this praise song to the tune of "The Farmer in the Dell."

sing Jesus is the king.
Jesus is the king.
We praise him with our song today.
Jesus is the king!

ask • How did the people in today's lesson praise Jesus?

• Why do you think it's important to sing praises to Jesus?

• How can we show Jesus that he is our king?

say The people in today's story rejoiced when Jesus came to their town. They were happy to see him. We show other people that Jesus is king when we worship him, give him our love, and tell others about him.

PRAYERS

Praise Prayer

Supplies: masking tape

Create a "road" with masking tape on the floor.

One at a time, have kids walk along the road and say one statement of praise they want to tell Jesus, such as "I love you for being my king," "Thanks for forgiving me," or "Thanks for loving me!" After everyone has had a chance to praise our king, Jesus, close by having everyone shout together:

PRay **We love you, Jesus!**

In Jesus' name, amen.

Praise You, Lord

Supplies: masking tape

Create a "road" with masking tape on the floor.

Have kids join you in singing this prayer to the tune of "Row, Row, Row Your Boat." Encourage children to walk down the road as they sing a prayer of praise to their Lord Jesus.

SING **Praise, praise, praise you, Lord.**

How wonderful you are!

And we want to give you praise.

We pray in Jesus' name.

Crunchy Path

Supplies: graham crackers, green-colored vanilla icing, M&M'S candies, teddy-bear crackers, plastic knives

Encourage kids to wash their hands before they prepare their snack, and make sure the snack table is clean. Have them each use a graham cracker to make a section of the road that Jesus and the donkey traveled. Have them spread icing on graham crackers, then place the graham crackers in a row on the table, as bricks on the road. Have children make a crowd by lining both sides of the road with teddy-bear crackers. Then have them drop M&M'S along the path as the donkey's footsteps.

Invite someone to say a prayer thanking Jesus for being our king. Then let kids eat the goodies!

"Praise the Lord" Snacks

Supplies: disposable tablecloth or plastic dropcloth, popped popcorn, two bowls

Have children wash their hands (or use wet wipes). Spread a large tablecloth or plastic dropcloth on the floor. Tell children that one way people celebrate is by throwing confetti. Explain that you've made some edible confetti! Give children one of the bowls of popcorn that you popped before class. Have kids stand on the tablecloth or plastic dropcloth. Encourage kids to take a handful of popcorn and throw it up high in the air! Let kids throw the popcorn for a few minutes. Then give children the other bowl of popcorn, and let them eat it. Ask a child to thank God for the snack and for sending his Son, Jesus, to earth to help us.

ask • **How do you think the people felt when they saw Jesus riding into town?**

• **How did the people praise Jesus?**

• **How can we praise Jesus?**

say Just as the people praised Jesus by waving palm branches and shouting "Hosanna!" we can praise Jesus, too, by telling other people about him, by worshipping him, and by praying to him. Jesus deserves our praise.

After the activity, roll up the tablecloth with the popcorn on it, and throw the tablecloth away.

SONGS

Royal Road

Supplies: masking tape, broom

Make a masking tape road on the floor. Provide a broom for the children to turn upside down and take turns riding as if it were a donkey.

Teach children the song "Jesus Came" to the tune of "Yankee Doodle." Then let kids take turns riding on the "donkey" up one side of the road and down the other side. Encourage the other children to follow behind and sing the song while marching and clapping. When everyone has had a turn riding the donkey, have the group sit in a circle.

SING Jesus came into the town
A-riding on a donkey.
Clap and sing and shout and praise
To Jesus who sure loves us!
Jesus Christ is Lord of all.
Jesus is our king!
Jesus Christ is Lord of all.
Jesus is our king!

Say It's fun to sing songs to Jesus. Jesus is the greatest king in the whole world, and we can give him our praises.

"Hosanna" Rhyme

Supplies: none

Have the children sit in a circle.

Say Let's think about the good things Jesus has done. Think about the things that make Jesus the best king there ever was.

Discuss the children's ideas for a minute or two. Then enjoy saying this rhyme together.

Have the child on your right say one good thing about Jesus, and then have the rest of the group chant, "Hosanna! Hosanna! Jesus is the king! Hosanna! Hosanna! Our praises we bring." Show the children how to clap after each "hosanna" and flutter-wave their hands during the line "Jesus is the king." Continue until each child has an opportunity to say one good thing about Jesus.

Jesus Washes the Disciples' Feet

Bible Basis:

John 13:1-17

Supplies:

Bible, dishpan of water, plastic baby doll, washcloth, towel

Open your Bible to John 13, and show children the words.

say ▶ **Today's Bible story tells us that God wants us to help others. So I want you to help me while I tell this story.**

One day Jesus was having a special dinner for his good friends. Let's set the table for the 12 disciples. Invite several children to pretend to set the table. **Thank you for helping—God wants us to help others.**

When Jesus' friends came for the dinner, they took off their shoes. Will you help me take off my shoes? Choose two children to help you remove your shoes.

The disciples' feet had gotten very dirty walking through the streets, because in those days people wore sandals, and the dirt roads could be very dusty. Most houses had servants who would help wash visitors' feet. Washing people's feet was not a fun job, and there were no servants at the place where Jesus and his friends were. But the disciples had to have their feet washed before dinner! Who would do it? Maybe one of the disciples? No way! It was a dirty job. Not one of the disciples wanted to wash the other disciples' feet. Jesus knew this would be a great time to teach his friends— and us, too—that God wants us to help others. Even though Jesus was the leader and teacher, he volunteered to wash the disciples' feet. Hold up the baby doll. **Let's wash this doll's feet to remember that we should help others like Jesus did.**

Put the dishpan of water in front of you. Allow children who haven't yet helped to take the washcloth and quickly wipe the doll's fee then dry its feet with the towel.

say ▶ **You've all done a very good job of helping me tell the Bible story. The story helps us remember that God wants us to help others.**

ask ▶ **• What did Jesus do that no one else wanted to do?**

• What are some other ways you can serve others?

say ▶ **Even though Jesus was a leader and teacher, he served his friends so that we would learn that God wants us to help others.**

PRAYERS

"First and Last" Prayer

Supplies: none

Have the children form a line. Let the last person in line come to the front of the line and say, "Dear God, help me to be first by serving others like Jesus did." When everyone has had a turn to say the prayer, end the prayer by saying, **"In Jesus' name, amen."**

SNACKS

Sweet Feet

Supplies: whipped topping, blue food coloring, spoon, paper plates, graham crackers

Stir a few drops of blue food coloring into a tub of non-dairy whipped topping. Let children pretend this is a basin of water. Give each child a dollop on his or her plate, then let children dip graham cracker squares into the whipped topping. Kids can pretend the crackers are dusty feet being cleaned in the blue water.

ask • **Do you think Jesus liked washing the feet of his friends? Why or why not?**

• **When do you think it's hard to help others? When is it easy?**

say **God wants us to help others, even if it's hard!**

Jesus came to Die for us

Bible Basis:

Luke 19:28-40; 23:1-49

Supplies:

Bible, coats, jackets, sweaters

Open your Bible to Luke 19, and show the children the words.

say ▶ **Today's Bible story tells us that Jesus died for us.**

Our Bible story begins as Jesus and his disciples were going from place to place preaching and teaching. When Jesus and his disciples were about to go into Jerusalem, Jesus sent his disciples ahead to get a young donkey that he could ride. During Bible times, kings and other royal people often rode donkeys to show that they would bring peace to the people. Jesus wanted to show that he was the King of kings. He was sent from God to bring peace and forgiveness for people's sins, as a prophet had promised a long time before.

ask ▶ **· How do you think the people felt to be so close to such an important person as Jesus?**

say ▶ **Show me how you think the people might have reacted when they saw Jesus coming.** Pause for the children to react. **The people were so excited to see Jesus that many of them threw their coats on the ground for the young donkey to walk on so he wouldn't get his hooves dirty. They treated Jesus like a king.**

We celebrate in many ways when someone does something extra special. We might cheer, clap, stomp our feet, or whistle. The people in Jesus' day did the same thing, and they celebrated with a procession or a parade. Let's act out a parade like the one the people had for Jesus.

Bring out the coats, jackets, and sweaters, and have each child choose an item to wear. Have children form groups with an even number in each group (four or six children to a group might work best). Let each of the groups choose a child to be the donkey and another child to be Jesus. Let the "Donkey" get on all fours, then have "Jesus" carefully sit on the Donkey's back. (If the floor is too hard, let Jesus simply put his or her hands on the Donkey's shoulders.) Let the other children each take off the clothing item and lay it on the floor in front of the Donkey. As each child puts his or her coat on the floor, have that child say something he or she likes about Jesus. Have the Donkey carry Jesus across the clothing, and then continue the Bible story.

say ▶ Many people were glad to see Jesus entering Jerusalem on a donkey. But some people were not happy to see Jesus. Some of the people were jealous and became angry with Jesus, so they asked the leaders to arrest him.

Jesus was arrested. The guards were mean, and they hurt Jesus very badly. Then they took Jesus to a man named Pilate who was kind of like the judges we have today. Pilate's job was to decide if Jesus had done anything wrong. The people said that Jesus had told everyone not to pay their taxes and that Jesus told people he was Christ, the King of kings.

ask ▶ • Do you think Jesus had done anything wrong? Why or why not?

say ▶ Pilate said that Jesus hadn't done anything wrong and that he should be set free, but the people were so angry that they wouldn't listen. Have kids put their hands over their ears, pretend not to listen, then take their hands away.

Pilate then sent Jesus to a man named Herod to let Herod decide what would happen to Jesus. Herod agreed that Jesus had done nothing to deserve death, but the angry crowd demanded that Jesus die.

ask ▶ • What would you have said to Herod or Pilate about Jesus?

say ▶ The people took Jesus to a hill with two criminals who had done some very bad things. The people hung Jesus on a cross to die alongside the criminals. They continued to call Jesus names and gave him vinegar to drink when he was thirsty. Jesus hung on the cross until he died.

ask ▶ • How do you think Jesus' friends felt when Jesus died?

say ▶ Even though dying on a cross was a terrible thing that happened to Jesus, Jesus knew God's plan. Just before Jesus died, he prayed and asked God to forgive all the people for their sins because they didn't realize what they were doing. Because Jesus died for us, our sins are forgiven and we can live with him in heaven. The most exciting part of God's plan for his Son was that Jesus didn't stay dead!

CRAFTS

A Bitter Drink for a King

Supplies: paper, markers, cotton swabs, vinegar, small bowls

Distribute the paper and markers. Instruct the kids to use the markers to draw a hill and a cross on the hill. Then have each of the children dip a cotton swab into a bowl of vinegar and dab the vinegar onto the cross.

say ▶ **The cross is a symbol that reminds us that Jesus died for our sins. This vinegar smells yucky—just like our sins are yucky to God. When Jesus died for our sins, he forgave us and he took away our yucky sins.**

ask ▶ **• What is something you've done that might make Jesus sad?**

• Have you asked Jesus to forgive your sins? Why or why not? Would you like to?

say ▶ **Even though some of the people were mean to Jesus, Jesus still loved the people and wanted God to forgive them. Jesus was willing to die on the cross for us and even for the sins of mean people. Jesus died for us.**

Cross Reminders

Supplies: wide crafts sticks (2 per child), glue, markers, clothespins (pinch kind), square note paper, magnetic tape

say ▶ **In today's lesson, we're learning that Jesus died for us. That's such an important thing to remember, let's make a craft that we'll see every day!**

Explain that people often write notes to help them remember important things. Say that kids will be making note holders to help them remember that Jesus died on the cross for us.

Give each child two wide craft sticks. Help kids use craft glue to attach the sticks in the shape of a cross. Help kids use markers to write "Jesus died for us" on their crosses.

Then give each child a wooden pinch clothespin, and use craft glue to attach the clothespin to the cross, pinch-side facing down. Give each child a small stack of square note paper, and help kids clip the paper in the clothespin. Finally, attach a strip of magnetic tape to the back of each cross.

say ▶ **Take these note holders home, and hang them on your refrigerators. That way, every time someone in your family writes a reminder note or opens the refrigerator, they'll remember that Jesus died for us!**

PRAYERS

Cloaks of Praise Prayer

Supplies: coats or dress-up clothes

Have children each choose a coat or other item of dress-up clothing and put on the item. Then instruct kids to take turns removing the items, laying them on the floor, and saying the following prayer.

PRay ▶ **Dear Jesus,**
Thank you for dying for me
And forgiving my sins.
In Jesus' name, amen.

snacks

Donkey Trail Mix

Supplies: paper towel, frosted-wheat cereal, cups, water

Have the children wash their hands (or use wet wipes), and then let kids sit down for their snacks. Remind the children that Jesus rode into Jerusalem on a young donkey. Tell kids that donkeys like to eat hay and drink lots of water.

Give children each a paper towel with a few frosted-wheat cereal pieces, and let kids pretend that the cereal is the donkey's hay. Then pass out cups of water. Let the children make donkey sounds while they wait for others to be served.

ask ▶ **· Do you think the donkey had any idea how special Jesus is? Why or**
why not?

say ▶ **The young donkey had a very special job to do for Jesus. Maybe**
he was rewarded with a special treat to eat. Let's eat our snack and
remember that soon after the donkey's special job was over, Jesus
would die for our sins. Bow your heads and let's pray.

Have the children repeat the following prayer before they eat their snacks.

PRay ▶ **Dear God, thank you for sending your Son, Jesus, to die for our sins.**
Bless this food. In Jesus' name, amen.

The Angel Frees Peter From Jail

Bible Basis:

 Acts 12:1-18

Supplies:

Bible; percussion instruments such as cymbals, triangles, or maracas

Pass out percussion instruments to the children. When the angel is mentioned in the story, have the children use the percussion instruments to make sounds of praise. Ask an adult or teenage volunteer to wait outside the door of your classroom so that the children can't see him or her. Tell the volunteer to enter the room when the children play the instruments while you're telling the story. Have your volunteer act out the angel's part of the story including touching Peter to wake him, repeating the words spoken by the angel, and disappearing at the end.

Open your Bible to Acts 12, and show the children the words.

say ▸ **Today's Bible story tells us that God's angels help us.**

Back when the disciples were telling people the wonderful news about Jesus, King Herod had many Christians arrested and thrown into jail. But Peter wasn't afraid, and he kept telling people about Jesus. Soon Peter was arrested, locked up in a jail cell, and guarded by soldiers.

Pick one child to be Peter, and tell the other children that they will pretend to be the guards. Have the "Guards" lock arms and stand in a circle with "Peter" in the center. Have Peter try to get out of the circle without running, jumping, or crawling.

ask ▸ **• How do you think you might escape from a locked room with guards watching you?**

• How do you think Peter felt when he was locked in jail?

Have the children sit in the circle. Have Peter remain in the center of the circle of Guards.

say ▸ **God's people prayed for Peter. They believed that God was powerful enough to free Peter from jail.**

The night before he was supposed to go to trial for believing in Jesus, Peter was chained up, sleeping between two soldiers. Have Peter pretend to be asleep.

Suddenly an angel appeared. Have kids play their instruments. The volunteer should enter the room and stand near the door. **And a bright light shone in the cell. The angel** (have kids play their instruments) **touched Peter on the side, woke him up, and said to him, "Peter, get up, put on your clothes and sandals, and follow me."** Have the person playing the angel repeat the words and act this out with Peter.

The chains fell away, and Peter followed the angel (have children play their instruments) **right out of the prison!** Have the volunteer bring Peter out from the center of the Guards. **When Peter and the angel got to the end of the street, the angel** (have children play their instruments) **left.** Have the person playing the angel disappear.

ask • **How did you feel when the surprise angel came in our room?**

• **How do you think Peter felt when the angel set him free?**

say When God's people pray, he hears them. And God's angels help us.

CRafts

A Special Appearance

Supplies: colored construction paper, lemon juice, bowl, cotton swabs, lamp with exposed 100-watt bulb

Distribute construction paper, and have children write their names on them. Pour lemon juice into a bowl, and give each child a cotton swab. Show children how to dip the cotton swabs into the lemon juice and use the swabs to draw angels on their paper. When the pictures have dried, show kids what happens when they hold their pictures about a half-inch away from a warm (100-watt) bulb. Move the paper over a bare bulb for about one minute, and then the picture will start to appear. Repeat with each child's paper.

ask • **How did you feel when the angel appeared on your paper?**

• **How is this like God surprising us with angels to help us?**

say God's angels are a little like the pictures you made—you can't always see angels, but they're still there. And God's angels help us by bringing God's protection and hope.

Prison Story Puppets

Supplies: plastic spoons, 3-inch squares of felt, chenille wire, fine-tip markers

Give each child two plastic spoons. Show children how to wrap a square of felt around the handle of a spoon and wrap a chenille wire around this to hold the "clothing" on the puppet. Children may use additional wires to make arms or other features. Let them use the markers to draw faces on their puppets. Encourage each child to make a Peter puppet and an angel puppet, then to retell the story with their puppets.

ask
- **Why do you think God used an angel to help Peter?**
- **How do you think God's angels might help you?**

say Use your puppets to tell someone at home the story we learned today. Be sure to share that God's angels help us.

Games

Peter, Peter, Angel

Supplies: none

Have children sit in a circle to play a game similar to Duck, Duck, Goose. One child will walk around the outside of the circle, tapping the children's heads and saying "Peter." When the child taps someone and says "angel," the Angel should get up, put an arm around the other child as if hugging him or her from the side, and walk around the circle once with the other child. Then the Angel becomes the Tapper. Continue until all children have been Tappers and Angels.

ask
- **How did the Angel keep you safe in our game?**
- **How did an angel keep Peter safe in our Bible story?**

say An angel opened the doors of the jail for Peter. In our game, the Angel held you while you walked around the circle. We can be sure that God's angels help us.

PRayeRS

Action Prayer

Supplies: angel figure

Have the children sit with you in a circle. Pass the angel around the circle. As children hold up the angel figure, have them repeat the following prayer.

PRay **Thank you, God, for sending angels to help us. In Jesus' name, amen.**

snacks

Angel Food Snacks

Supplies: plastic tablecloth, food coloring, small bowls, angel food cake, angel-shaped cookie cutter, clean paintbrushes

Have children wash their hands. Cover a table with a plastic tablecloth, and place small amounts of food coloring in bowls on the table.

Give each child a piece of angel food cake. Let kids take turns using an angel-shaped cookie cutter to cut out angel shapes from the pieces of cake. Then have kids each use a clean paintbrush and food coloring to paint a face on the angel.

ask **· Why do you think God sends angels?**

say **When we're scared, we can remember that God is with us. When we need help, God's angels help us.** When kids have finished making their snacks, ask a volunteer to pray for the snack.

Angel Apple Snacks

Supplies: plates, apple slices, pretzel rods

Have the children wash their hands (or use wet wipes) and then sit down to prepare their snack. Distribute a plate, two apple sections, and a large pretzel rod to each child. Show children how to set the pretzel rod in the middle of the plate, then place the apple sections on both sides of the pretzel rod as "angel wings."

ask **· How did an angel help Peter?**

· How can angels help us?

say **God sent an angel to help Peter, and God's angels help us, too. Let's thank God for sending angels to help us and for providing our snack.** Invite one child to pray for the snack.

LyDia Is ConVeRteD

Bible Basis:

Acts 16:9-16

Supplies:

Bible, paper heart with "Jesus Loves You" written on it, blue blanket or towel

Open your Bible to Acts 16, and show the children the words.

say **Today's Bible story tells us that everyone needs Jesus. We'll hear about how a man named Paul told people about Jesus. I'd like you to help me act out this Bible story.**

Have the children form two groups. Place a blue blanket or towel between the two groups, and explain that the blue blanket is a "river." Choose one child to be Paul, and choose a child from the other group to be Lydia. Explain that Lydia was a merchant who sold expensive purple cloth.

say **One day Paul was praying.** Have "Paul" and the other children in Paul's group kneel as if praying. **While he was praying, he had a dream. A man from a faraway place said, "Come here and help us!"** Have "Lydia" and the other children in Lydia's group cup their hands around their mouths and call out, "Come here and help us!" **The people didn't know about Jesus. Paul wanted to tell the people, "Jesus loves you!" So Paul decided to take his important message to the people of the faraway place.**

Give Paul the heart. Tell the children that Paul traveled across water to get to the faraway place, and then have the children in Paul's group walk across the blanket to reach Lydia's group. Ask the children from both groups to shake hands and greet each other and then sit down.

say **Paul told the people about Jesus.** Have the children from Paul's group take turns saying, "Everyone needs Jesus."

A woman named Lydia wanted to know Jesus. Have Lydia and Paul stand up. Ask Paul to give the heart to Lydia. Paul told Lydia, "Jesus loves you!" **Lydia and her whole family decided to love Jesus, too. They learned that everyone needs Jesus.** Have children stand up and cheer. Set aside the heart.

ask • **How do you think Lydia felt when she learned that Jesus loved her?**

• **Why did Paul want to tell others about Jesus?**

say ▶ **Some people don't know that Jesus loves them. Isn't that sad? Paul wanted the people to know about Jesus. Paul wanted them to know that everyone needs Jesus. We can tell people about Jesus' love, too.**

BiBLe eXPeRieNCeS

Everyone Needs Jesus

Supplies: masking tape, magazine pictures of people, wooden blocks

Place small pieces of masking tape (about 1½ inches long) on the edge of a table, and show kids how to roll the pieces of tape, sticky side out, to attach the magazine pictures to wooden blocks so the figures stand up.

Have kids use extra blocks or other items in the classroom to build a marketplace where the block people can buy and sell things such as pieces of fabric, miniature toy animals, or food items. As the children re-create a marketplace like the one in which Lydia may have sold her goods, encourage kids to pretend to be Lydia or another merchant. Other children might pretend to be Paul and tell their friends what they know about Jesus and that everyone needs Jesus.

ask ▶ • **Where are some places that you could tell people about Jesus?**

• **What would you tell someone about Jesus?**

say ▶ **Jesus wants us to tell people that they need him. Jesus has done so much for us, and he wants to do the same for others. We should tell everyone that they can believe in Jesus and be saved.**

CRafts

A Church for Jesus

Supplies: newspaper, white construction paper, pencils, glue, straws of candy powder

Cover a table with newspaper. Set out the other supplies.

say ▶ **God sent Paul to Macedonia to tell everyone the good news about Jesus. Because Paul obeyed God, Lydia and the people in Macedonia learned about Jesus. Now Christians meet in buildings called "churches" all over the world to share how the good news of Jesus has changed their lives.**

First, have kids each use a pencil to draw a church building on the construction paper. Then they can rub the glue onto different areas of the church and sprinkle powdered candy over the glue, as you would sprinkle glitter, to decorate their churches.

ask ▶ **• Why do you think we build churches today?**

• Who could you invite to come to our church?

say ▶ **A church building is a place where people can come together to celebrate the good news of Jesus. We can make a church building from wood or bricks—but we can tell people the good news about Jesus wherever we are, just like Paul and his friends did.**

Prayer Picture Frames

Supplies: craft foam, glue, scraps of yarn, self-adhesive magnet strips

Give each child a 5x7-inch sheet of craft foam. Help children glue colorful scraps of yarn to the border of the foam to make a frame. Place a self-adhesive magnet strip on the back of each frame. Explain that each child can glue a picture of someone who needs Jesus into the frame when he or she gets home and then put this on the refrigerator as a reminder to pray for that person.

ask ▶ **• Who is someone you know who needs Jesus?**

• How will you pray for this person?

say ▶ **Everyone needs Jesus, and God can use your prayers to help someone get to know Jesus!**

Games

Sailing Ships

Supplies: 2 buckets or tubs filled with water, plastic boats

Gather children together in front of a table. Set out two buckets or tubs filled with water. Give children plastic boats to play with in the water. Have them pair up and work to get the boat from one side of the tub to the other without touching the boat. Show them how to blow the boat to move it on the water.

ask
- **How did Paul get to the faraway place?**
- **Why did he go to the faraway place?**

say Paul got on a boat to go to a faraway place to tell everyone there about Jesus. We can tell our friends at school, day care, and at home about Jesus. We know, just as Paul did, that everyone needs Jesus.

Prayers

Good News Prayer

Supplies: pictures of people cut from magazines

Have kids sit in a circle, and place the pictures in the center of the circle.

say Pretend the pictures are of people we know who we can tell about Jesus. Close your eyes and think of one good thing you know about Jesus, then open your eyes. We're going to take turns around the circle choosing a magazine picture and handing the picture to a classroom friend in our circle. When you hand the picture to your friend, tell him or her the good thing you know about Jesus, then sit back down. Let the child on your left go first, then have each child choose another child to tell about Jesus. When everyone who wants to has participated, lead kids in saying the following prayer.

pray Dear God,
Thank you for helping me tell everyone
The good news about Jesus.
In Jesus' name, amen.

Sharing Jesus

Supplies: paper heart

Explain that you'll start a prayer, then you'll pause so children can take turns saying the name of someone they want to tell about Jesus. Tell children that you'll pass the heart around the circle. When the heart comes to a child, he or she can say the name of the person the child wants to tell about Jesus, and then give the heart to the next child.

PRay ▶ **Dear God, we know that everyone needs Jesus. It makes us sad to think about the people who don't know how much you love us. Please help us tell these people about Jesus.**

Say the name of a person you want to tell about Jesus, then pass the heart to a child. When everyone has had a chance to say a name, close the prayer.

In Jesus' name, amen.

snacks

Purple Pops

Supplies: paper plates, marshmallows, pretzel sticks, purple grape juice, cups

Have the children wash their hands (or use wet wipes) before they begin making the snacks. Give each child a plate with two large marshmallows and two large pretzel sticks, plus a small cup of purple grape juice. Ask one of the children to thank God for providing today's snacks.

Show kids how to create Purple Pops by placing a large marshmallow on the end of a pretzel stick. Let kids discover what happens when they dip their marshmallows into the grape juice. Remind kids that Lydia is remembered in the Bible for being one of the first women in Macedonia (a part of Europe today) to hear the good news about Jesus.